INFUSED WATER

100 Easy, Delicious Recipes for Detox, Weight Loss, Healthy Skin, Better Immunity, and More!

Britt Brandon, CFNS, CPT

Aadamsmedia
Avon, Massachusetts

Published by
Adams Media, a division of F+W Media, Inc.
57 Littlefield Street, Avon, MA 02322. U.S.A.
www.adamsmedia.com

ISBN 10: 1-4405-9470-8
ISBN 13: 978-1-4405-9470-0
eISBN 10: 1-4405-9471-6
eISBN 13: 978-1-4405-9471-7

Printed in the United States of America.

10   9   8   7   6   5   4   3   2   1

Library of Congress Cataloging-in-Publication Data
Brandon, Britt, author.
Infused water / Britt Brandon.
Avon, Massachusetts: Adams Media, [2016]
LCCN 2015043720 (print) | LCCN 2015044592 (ebook) | ISBN
   9781440594700 (pb) | ISBN 1440594708 (pb) | ISBN
   9781440594717 (ebook) | ISBN 1440594716 (ebook)
LCSH: Herbal teas. | Flavoring essences. | Functional foods. |
   Drinking water. | Water--Health aspects. | Hydrotherapy. | BISAC: COOKING
   / Beverages / General. | COOKING / Health & Healing / General. | COOKING /
   Specific Ingredients / Fruit. | LCGFT: Cookbooks.
LCC TX817.T3 B73 2016 (print) | LCC TX817.T3 (ebook) | DDC
   613.2/87--dc23
LC record available at *http://lccn.loc.gov/2015043720*

Cover design and photography by Stephanie Hannus.

This book is available at quantity discounts for bulk purchases.
For information, please call 1-800-289-0963.

Contents

Introduction

In recent decades, the glass of thirst-quenching water has slowly been replaced by sugary alternatives such as sodas and sweetened fruit juices. Concerned by the increase of conditions related to sugary drink consumption, many people have started opting for the pure hydration that can only be found with water. Replacing sugary drinks with water has helped many people in their efforts to lose weight and live healthier lives by avoiding the catastrophic illnesses and conditions that can result from the overwhelming amounts of sugar and chemicals in the standard diet. While major threats to health loom in every glass of synthetic juices, sodas, and drinks, there is a more serious (and far more common) condition that can develop in just a few hours without water, producing symptoms many people ignore. Most people simply dismiss their daily dips in energy, mental "fogginess," unexplained hunger, and even irritability and mood swings on the blood sugar spikes and dips that sugary drink consumption inevitably causes. Surprisingly, though, these experiences are more likely symptoms of a far more serious condition: dehydration.

The average person's daily water consumption falls short of the widely accepted recommendation of 64 ounces, with some folks drinking little to no water at all. The most common reason people don't choose water is the "plainness" of water. In contrast to the synthetically formulated sugary beverages they normally drink, water seems to lack flavor. But what if there was a delicious way to add water to your day that not only brightened every glass with vibrant color, but also added vital nutrients that help your body to function and thrive? While this may sound too good to be true, there is such a creation, and you can make it right in your own home simply and easily. Introducing: *infused water*!

By adding slices and bits of your favorite fruit combinations, fragrant herbs, and other simple ingredients, you can create pitchers of water that make a daily water habit more delicious (and nutritious) than ever before. Flavored with sweet, spicy, or savory combinations of vibrant fruits and vegetables, you can get out of the "plain water" rut and start succeeding at your water intake goals every single day.

Consuming adequate amounts of water will boost everything from your skin health to your brain function. With the array of benefits you can reap from adding fruits, vegetables, and other extras, your water becomes packed with vitamins, minerals, and phytochemicals that can help you achieve a variety of health goals with every single sip!

This book provides you with 100 detailed infused water recipes that combine your favorite fruits, vegetables, herbs, and spices to create drinks that not only taste great but also help you achieve better overall health. So, whether your goal is to increase energy, improve immunity, lose weight, fight chronic disease, or aid digestion, you can combine specific ingredients in your water to produce the very benefits you seek . . . simply and deliciously!

Chapter 1

Essential Hydration for Health

We've all heard how important it is to remain hydrated. Our parents, coaches, and trusted physicians have spent years preaching the importance of water's hydration, and it turns out they were right all along! Whether you're moving through your normal everyday routine or hitting it hard in the gym, the body needs water in order to function. Most people admit that they rarely consume the accepted daily recommendation of eight (8-ounce) glasses of water, opting instead for tasty treats such as sugary drinks. When it comes to hydration, though, those sugary drinks don't cut it. When you discover the importance of hydration, and learn how water truly supports your body's parts and processes and how dehydration in even the mildest form can adversely affect your body's functioning, you may just start sipping your water a little more regularly. Luckily, with the addition of infused water to your daily routine, you can enjoy delicious and nutritious water that not only tastes great, but also hydrates your body so it can function at its very best.

The Importance of Hydration

When we're born, our bodies are composed of about 75 percent water. As we age, that percentage drops to about 65 percent (about two-thirds of our body's weight), and varies depending upon age, sex, and muscle and fat percentages. Containing essential nutrients that the body requires in order to perform everyday functions, water is the clean hydration our bodies need in order to survive and thrive. Replenishing the body's cells, organs, and systems with adequate hydration is imperative, and while many people quench their thirst with sugary synthetic beverages such as sodas and sweetened fruit juices, these drinks offer little in terms of hydration and a great deal in terms of harm. When the essential nutrients provided by water are replaced with synthetic additives, empty calories, and loads of sugar, the brain and body reap none of the benefits that water provides, and instead endure blood sugar spikes and crashes, overwhelming processing and storage of improper "nutrients" (what some might refer to as "malnutrients"), and (of course) inadequate hydration. All of these malnutrients wreak havoc on the body's brain, cells, organs, and systems, compromising the body's functions rather than supporting them. If you don't think water is overly important for the body's proper functioning, simply take a look at what water does for the body.

Physical Processes That Depend upon Adequate Hydration

Adequate hydration is essential to the optimal performance of every process in the body and the functioning of every cell, organ, and system. Clearly, a focus on consuming enough water daily is a step in the right direction toward achieving overall health. "To think, drink, and blink, you need water" is a saying that sums up the body's needs for hydration in order to perform every function, whether simple or complex, voluntary or involuntary. Water supports the electrical impulses that allow the heart to beat, the nerves and spinal cord to communicate, and the brain to process information. To move, jump, throw, and perform any physical activity, the body's muscles need water. The joints, eyes, nose, and mouth are lubricated by (you guessed it) water. In addition to all the benefits that result from hydrating the body's cells and systems, your brain and body experience far fewer difficulties thanks to the improved detoxification, proper digestion, and enhanced nutrient absorption that naturally occur when the body has adequate amounts of water.

The Average Person's Water Needs

The average person doesn't consume enough water on a daily basis. Most people are simply unaware of how little water it takes to actually keep the body hydrated and operating at its best. In order to perform everyday functions such as breathing and muscle movement, and involuntary actions including digestion and heartbeats, the body requires about 2 liters of water per day (about 68 ounces or about 8½ cups). Those 2 liters of water help the body perform everyday functions, and replenish the stores of water that are constantly escaping the body through every exhaled breath, urination, and perspiration. Factors such as sex, age, and body composition (the ratio of fat to muscle percentage) play into the amount of water needed by the body on a daily basis, but the fluctuation is minimal, making the general rule of eight (8-ounce) cups per day widely accepted for the general population over the age of eighteen. There are instances when the amount of water required by the body increases, such as with an increase of physical activity, extended exposure to hot and/or humid climates, and illnesses that can lead to fluid loss, such as those that occur with vomiting and diarrhea.

Those eight cups of water can be consumed during a twelve-hour period by simply drinking a single cup every hour and a half. Dividing the total daily amount into regular "doses" lets the body achieve and maintain adequate hydration throughout the day. Energy levels, focus, digestion, and even mood can remain unaffected by the effects of dehydration. Making it even easier to fulfill those hourly water intake goals are the sweet treats that can be concocted with this book's infused water recipes, but more on that later.

The Process and Effects of Dehydration

Most people have experienced the dry mouth or slight twinge of a headache that usually signals the need for water, but few people are aware of the actual process that takes us to the point of dehydration. It all starts with the hypothalamus, the gland responsible for a number of functions, including:

- Hormone production
- Body temperature regulation
- Constant evaluation and maintenance of the body's fluid balance

All three of these functions play roles in the process of keeping the body hydrated. When the hypothalamus detects too little water in the blood, it signals to the pituitary gland to release an anti-diuretic hormone (ADH). The ADH signals the kidneys to minimize their process of removing water from the blood while returning as much fluid as possible into the bloodstream. Once the kidneys pump the brakes on water extraction and instead focus on returning water content to the blood, the need to urinate lessens and urine becomes more concentrated (thus the dark yellow hue that is a common indicator of dehydration). Once this process has reached a point where the blood volume is adversely affected, the brain signals thirst, and you feel the urge to drink. If the process is prolonged, the percentage of water in the blood drops, leading to a reduced blood volume; this in turn leads to a drop in blood pressure and an increase in heart rate, both of which are detrimental to all of the cells, as well as the organs and systems throughout the body. As the process of becoming dehydrated continues to pile stress on the cardiovascular system, the supply and delivery of oxygen to the brain is reduced, resulting in headaches, fatigue, inability to concentrate, and fluctuations in mood. Once water is consumed, though, the body is able to replenish the blood, cells, organs, and systems with the hydration they require, and the body can function as intended again.

Side Effects and Symptoms of Dehydration

Dehydration ranges on a scale from mild to severe, with symptoms and consequences ranging in severity between those two extremes. In mild to moderate dehydration that can result from strenuous or prolonged activity, extended heat exposure, or illnesses and conditions that involve fluid loss (high fever, vomiting, and/or diarrhea), one of the first indications of the need for water is thirst. As dehydration ensues, the following symptoms are commonly reported:

- Dry mouth
- Swollen tongue
- Fatigue
- Decrease in urination frequency
- Headache
- Dry skin
- Dizziness
- Hunger

If the dehydration becomes severe, the signs and symptoms change to include indications that serious damage to the organs and systems is setting in. If you begin to experience these symptoms or are in the presence of someone else exhibiting the symptoms, water should be consumed immediately, and you should seek emergency assistance. The following are symptoms of moderate to severe dehydration:

- Fever at or above 103°F
- Confusion
- Lethargy
- Seizures
- Difficulty breathing
- Chest pain or abdominal pain
- Fainting
- No urine for twelve hours or more

Chapter 2

Introducing Water Infusion

With all of the hype surrounding infused waters, it's no wonder that more and more people are becoming interested in the delicious and nutritious alternative to a plain glass of water. With the endorsement of popular physicians like Dr. Oz, countless celebrities, and even grocery chains that have started providing infused water products directly to consumers, infused water is no longer seen as a "fad" but rather as a health movement that is helping to improve the quality of life for people around the globe. The easy infusion process starts with a variety of fruits, vegetables, or herbs of your choosing, and because you're able to use combinations of your favorite produce, you'll find making your daily water intake goals even easier to achieve.

What Is Infusion?

Infusion is defined by Oxford Dictionary as "a drink, remedy, or extract prepared by soaking the leaves of a plant or herb in liquid and allowing the materials to remain suspended in the liquid for a certain amount of time," or "the introduction of a new element or quality into something." The method of infusing water with the essences of delicious additions was thought to be born in 2737 B.C.E., and this first recorded infusion happened by sheer accident. Legend has it that the first infusion occurred when dried tea leaves accidently fell into the steaming hot cup of water belonging to the Chinese emperor, Shen Nung. When these leaves were added to the hot water, the color, flavor, aroma, and nutrients were released from the leaves, infusing that first cup of water and beginning a tradition that would eventually take the world by storm.

Over the centuries, teas, tinctures, and tonics have grown in popularity, resulting in an ever-growing variety of infused products that include everything from herb-infused massage oils to infused drinking waters. With infusion, anyone can take a simple cup of pure water to new taste-sensation heights. Whether you choose herbs, fruits, vegetables, or a combination, the infusion method allows you to transform your water into a delicious, nutritious alternative that packs flavor and nutrients into every sip.

Creating your infusions is quick and easy. Once you determine which additions you will use to infuse your water, a simple peel, slice, or chop is all it takes for preparation. After your produce is prepped, add cool distilled, filtered, or spring water and let the mixture blend. Within just a few hours in the refrigerator or on your countertop, your water is infused with the flavors and nutrients of each addition you choose. For best results, it is recommended that you use fresh or frozen fruits for your infusions, and always remember to discard the infusion additions afterward. In order to preserve the freshness of your fruits and infusion, it is best to refrigerate your infusions after the first few hours, if you choose to set your infusion on the countertop initially.

The Benefits of Infused Water

Something as simple as infused water may seem to have a minimal effect on health, but nothing could be further from the truth. While smoothies and juices can be heavy and filling, infused water offers a lighter alternative that not only hydrates but supplies the body with essential nutrients for optimal functioning and improved overall health. Instead of sugary juices, your infused water can offer a refreshing alternative that not only tastes great, but provides a wide variety of vitamins, minerals, and phytochemicals. With vitamins like A, Bs, C, and E; minerals like calcium, potassium, magnesium, and zinc; and phytochemicals that serve as potent protective and preventative antioxidants, your infused waters can help you achieve greater health in every area. Everything from improved digestion, easier weight loss, and healthier skin to boosted energy and more effective immunity can be achieved with the simple addition of infused waters to your diet. Harnessing the power of the potent nutrients naturally provided by fresh produce, infused waters can transform your health and your life—one delicious and healthful sip at a time!

What Equipment Do You Need?

Creating your own unique infused water recipes is as easy as a quick peel, cut, or slice. With the fruits, vegetables, and herbs that are readily available at your local grocery store, you can turn countless combinations into infused water recipes. Peeling your favorite citrus, apples, and pears; slicing delightfully delicious pineapples and kiwis; and muddling fresh berries of every color takes only a matter of minutes. You can create batches of tasty and nutritious infused water using only these few tools:

- A small paring knife
- A simple cutting board
- A pitcher that can hold at least 1½ liters of water (allowing for 1 liter water and adequate space for your healthful additions)

Your infused water develops in a mere few hours of steeping in your refrigerator or on your countertop. Any of the water that you don't drink on the day you make it should have the additions removed from the pitcher and then can be stored in the refrigerator for up to three days. By preparing your infusions the night before, you can allow the additions to infuse the water fully overnight for the perfect concoction ready to sip by the next morning.

Infusion Products Available

Though not necessary, some handy water infusion products are available for purchase. Specially designed pitchers and bottles have a removable canister to hold the additions you place into the batch of infused water. These pitchers and bottles, costing about $15 and up, help make your infused water preparation neat and easy, but, again, they are not necessary. Any container, from a mason jar to a simple pitcher, can be used to create infused waters. You don't even need refrigeration; the process of infusion can take place on your countertop. The only equipment required is a knife to peel, cut, chop, or slice, and a simple container to hold the ingredients.

Nutrition Made Simple

Not surprisingly, the majority of people don't consume anywhere near the recommended daily 64 ounces of water. The most commonly cited reason for not drinking enough water is the lack of taste. Because our taste buds have been conditioned by the bombardment of sugary beverages, the average person opts for sodas, juices, and unhealthy sugar-laden beverages that not only contribute nothing to the body's nutritional requirements but exacerbate multiple health complications, including diabetes and obesity. Infused waters can even be consumed as the healthier alternative to coffee and energy drinks, helping to stimulate the senses and rejuvenate body and mind healthfully.

With infused waters, the plain, uninviting glass of water can be transformed into a flavorful, nutritious beverage that makes achieving the daily 64-ounce goal a pleasure. These delicious treats not only help with hydration, but provide a nutritious low-calorie alternative to sweetened fruit juices. Drinking pure water infused with your favorite natural fruits and seasonings will be one of the easiest lifestyle changes you can make. Expect a dramatic impact on everything from digestion and immunity to skin tone and weight loss. Infused waters can transform your health and your life!

Chapter 3

Infusions for Detoxification

Whether you're looking for the perfect drink to sip throughout your cleanse or simply seeking a daily drink that offers detoxification benefits, these recipes for infused waters are perfect for your wants and needs. Subtle enough to be sipped throughout the day, these blends of fruit-, vegetable-, and herb-infused waters help flush your cells, organs, and systems of the toxins and impurities that can wreak havoc on your body. Filled with potent antioxidants, vitamins, minerals, and phytochemicals, as well as providing natural toxin-foraging benefits, these delicious infused waters also transform a plain cup of water into a sensational taste experience. With less toxicity, the body and brain are able to function as designed, leading to better health and an improved quality of life.

The Healthy Master Cleanse

The Master Cleanse is one of the best-known cleanses used for detoxification. Safe, easy, and delicious, this delightful (yet slightly spicy!) spin on a proven cleanse can make your daily water servings do double duty as hydrating helpings that also work to detoxify your brain and body.

Ingredients | Yields 1 liter

1 liter water
1 large lemon, peeled and sliced
1 teaspoon red pepper flakes, prepared in a spice bag
1 organic green tea bag

1. Prepare a pitcher or water infuser product with 1 liter water.

2. Place the lemon slices, spice bag, and green tea bag inside the pitcher or water infuser's canister.

3. Allow mixture to steep in the refrigerator or a cool, dark place for 2–4 hours. For best flavor and health benefits, consume within 24–48 hours.

The Key Ingredients

The ingredients in this water are detoxification stars. The vitamin C–rich lemon is a powerful purifier for the blood and organs, and helps purge the body of impurities while supporting the liver and kidneys. The red pepper flakes lend a metabolism-boosting kick that helps the body pump blood and remove toxins and impurities at a faster rate. The green tea helps provide the body with potent phytochemicals and polyphenols such as catechins that act as powerful antioxidants, helping support the immune system as the detoxification process progresses.

Mango-Ginger with Berries

This infused water recipe packs a variety of flavors and even more nutrients into every last sip so you can detoxify deliciously! The ginger in this recipe will increase your energy and help you fight the commonly reported fatigue that can result from detoxification.

Ingredients | Yields 1 liter
1 liter water
½ large mango, peeled and sliced
½ cup raspberries, muddled
1 tablespoon peeled and sliced ginger

1. Prepare a pitcher or water infuser product with 1 liter water.

2. Place the mango slices, raspberries (and juice), and ginger inside the pitcher or water infuser's canister.

3. Allow mixture to steep in the refrigerator or a cool, dark place for 4–8 hours. For best flavor and health benefits, consume within 24–48 hours.

The Key Ingredients

Featuring mangoes packed with beta-carotene, a powerful polyphenol and antioxidant that gives the fruit its beautiful hue, this blend protects the cells from free radical damage and oxidative stress, and helps to purge toxins from the bloodstream. Raspberries not only add to the immunity-boosting benefit with their anthocyanins that act as potent antioxidants, but also help to fight bacteria that can linger in the blood and digestive system. The potent spiciness of the ginger speeds metabolism, prevents infection, and increases energy.

Minty Grapefruit

This delightfully delicious combination of citrus spiced with mint and ginger makes the perfect thirst-quenching recipe for detoxification success! The lemon and lime in this recipe help relieve the pain and pressure of inflammation, and combine to combat toxic buildup and irritation that can otherwise prevent the organs from functioning as designed.

Ingredients | Yields 1 liter

1 liter water
½ medium pink grapefruit, peeled and sliced
½ large lemon, peeled and sliced
½ large lime, peeled and sliced
1 tablespoon mint leaves, crushed
1" piece ginger, peeled and sliced

1. Prepare a pitcher or water infuser product with 1 liter water.

2. Place the grapefruit, lemon, lime, mint, and ginger inside the pitcher or water infuser's canister.

3. Allow mixture to steep in the refrigerator or a cool, dark place for 4–8 hours. For best flavor and health benefits, consume within 24–48 hours.

The Key Ingredients

The vitamin C–rich grapefruit contains lycopene, which not only acts as a potent antioxidant for cell health and cell regeneration but also helps to regulate blood pressure. The lemon and lime contribute limonoids, which help to combat free radical damage to cells and help to relieve inflammation, one of the major causes of pain in the body's joints and extremities. The mint and ginger contribute enzymes, oils, and polyphenols that help the functioning of the cardiovascular system, immune system, and nervous system.

Spiced Lemon-Lime

Calming the bitter taste of green tea while complementing the tart flavor of the apple cider vinegar, the citrus fruits of this infusion not only contribute delicious flavor but also benefit the body and mind with potent nutrition that supports the body's healthy functioning and detoxifies the body deliciously.

Ingredients | Yields 1 liter
1 liter water
1 large lemon, peeled and sliced
1 large lime, peeled and sliced
2 organic green tea bags
1 tablespoon organic, unfiltered, unpasteurized apple cider vinegar

1. Prepare a pitcher or water infuser product with 1 liter water.

2. Place the lemon, lime, tea bags, and vinegar inside the pitcher or water infuser's canister.

3. Allow mixture to steep in the refrigerator or a cool, dark place for 4–8 hours. For best flavor and health benefits, consume within 24–48 hours.

The Key Ingredients

Vitamin C in the lemon and lime acts as a powerful antioxidant that protects the cells, organs, and systems against harmful free radical damage and oxidative stress while also cleansing the blood of toxins. Further supporting the efforts of the vitamin C are the naturally occurring enzymes and potent catechins of the apple cider vinegar and green tea. Helping to combat inflammation, infection, and cellular degradation, these ingredients combine to create a sweet yet subtle green tea infusion that maximizes your detoxification benefits.

Lemon-Cranberry Dandelion Tea

Renowned as a beneficial blend of ingredients, this recipe's combination of sweet citrus, tart cranberries, and detoxifying dandelion tea makes for a delicious way to cleanse the body.

Ingredients | Yields 1 liter

1 liter water
1 large lemon, peeled and sliced
½ cup cranberries, crushed
1 dandelion tea bag

1. Prepare a pitcher or water infuser product with 1 liter water.

2. Place the lemon, cranberries (and juice), and tea bag inside the pitcher or water infuser's canister.

3. Allow mixture to steep in the refrigerator or a cool, dark place for 4–8 hours. For best flavor and health benefits, consume within 24–48 hours.

The Key Ingredients

Maximizing benefits to the entire body, the potent antioxidants in these ingredients combine to combat infection, inflammation, and the oxidative stress that can lead to chronic illness and disease. Supporting the immune system, cardiovascular system, nervous system, and cognitive processes, vitamin C, B vitamins, calcium, magnesium, and powerful antioxidants infuse this delicious recipe with health benefits that not only detoxify and protect against harmful toxins, but make achieving your daily goal of water consumption easier than ever!

Strawberry-Pineapple

With nutrients including B vitamins, vitamin C, magnesium, and potassium, this infused water recipe delivers all of the essentials needed to maintain a detoxification program that's not only nutritious, but delicious, too!

Ingredients | Yields 1 liter

1 liter water
6 strawberries, tops removed and sliced
2 (¾"-thick) slices of pineapple, peeled and chopped
2 tablespoons whole basil leaves
1 tablespoon organic, unfiltered, unpasteurized apple cider vinegar

1. Prepare a pitcher or water infuser product with 1 liter water.

2. Place the strawberries, pineapple, basil, and vinegar inside the pitcher or water infuser's canister.

3. Allow mixture to steep in the refrigerator or a cool, dark place for 4–8 hours. For best flavor and health benefits, consume within 24–48 hours.

The Key Ingredients

Strawberries and pineapple not only contribute a sensational sweetness to this infusion but also provide the body with an astounding amount of nutrients that work together to combat illness, protect cellular health, promote proper system functioning, and detoxify the body of impurities. Infusing every sip with vibrant colors and flavors, these two ingredients provide the body with plentiful antioxidants that forage free radicals, fight toxicity, and prevent oxidative damage to the cells, organs, and systems that are responsible for detoxification.

Raspberry-Lime with Mint

Visually appealing, the red raspberries pair up with vibrant green limes and mint leaves to create a delicious combination of potent ingredients that provide powerful nutrients including B vitamins, vitamins A, C, and E, calcium, magnesium, and antioxidants galore!

Ingredients | Yields 1 liter
1 liter water
½ cup raspberries, muddled
1 large lime, peeled and chopped
2 tablespoons whole mint leaves

1. Prepare a pitcher or water infuser product with 1 liter water.

2. Place the raspberries (and juice), lime, and mint inside the pitcher or water infuser's canister.

3. Allow mixture to steep in the refrigerator or a cool, dark place for 4–8 hours. For best flavor and health benefits, consume within 24–48 hours.

The Key Ingredients

The anthocyanins that color raspberries their delightful shade of red team up with the lignin of the limes and the natural oils of mint to act as potent cell-protecting agents that not only safeguard the health of cells, but also contribute to the detoxification of the blood, body, and brain. Scouring free radicals, removing toxins, and eliminating the impurities that can wreak havoc on the functioning of the body, this recipe's ingredients not only look and taste great, but also help you feel great!

Peachy Cherry with Ginger

Sweet peaches, tart cherries, and spicy ginger team up in this detoxifying recipe for a sensational taste that makes it easy to achieve proper hydration, detoxification, and optimal levels of health deliciously.

Ingredients | Yields 1 liter

1 liter water
1 large peach, peeled, pitted, and sliced
½ cup pitted cherries, chopped
1" piece ginger, peeled and sliced

1. Prepare a pitcher or water infuser product with 1 liter water.

2. Place the peaches, cherries, and ginger inside the pitcher or water infuser's canister.

3. Allow mixture to steep in the refrigerator or a cool, dark place for 4–8 hours. For best flavor and health benefits, consume within 24–48 hours.

The Key Ingredients

This infused water recipe provides detoxifying nutrients such as vitamin C and potent phytochemicals such as anthocyanins, beta-carotene, and a number of enzymes and oils. Scouring the body in search of toxins, free radicals, and other harmful compounds, these ingredients' potent nutrients make detoxification simple and delicious. Not only is this blend of bright peaches, deep red cherries, and beautiful ginger a feast for the eyes, it pleases the palate, prevents toxicity, protects the body's cells, organs, and systems against harm, and promotes overall health and well-being.

Crisp Cranberry-Lime

Helping to protect the entire body against the toxins that promote free radical damage, while supporting the immune system and protecting against illness and disease, these ingredients combine to create a beautiful infusion that benefits overall health with every delicious sip.

Ingredients | Yields 1 liter

1 liter water
½ cup cranberries, crushed
1 large lime, peeled and sliced
1" piece ginger, peeled and sliced

1. Prepare a pitcher or water infuser product with 1 liter water.
2. Place the cranberries (and juice), lime, and ginger inside the pitcher or water infuser's canister.
3. Allow mixture to steep in the refrigerator or a cool, dark place for 4–8 hours. For best flavor and health benefits, consume within 24–48 hours.

The Key Ingredients

Crisp cranberries contribute far more than just a flavorful deliciousness to this infused water recipe. Cranberries' antibacterial, antiviral, and antimicrobial benefits support the immune system, safeguard the cells, organs, and systems, and specifically target the barrage of toxins that can wreak havoc on everything from the urinary tract to the cardiovascular system. These beautiful berries combine with vitamin C–rich lime that provides its own sensational citrus flavor and a host of antioxidants to benefit the body in an astounding number of ways.

Blueberry-Orange

This tangy blend of fruits contains supportive nutrients that specifically promote the health and proper functioning of the liver, making for the perfect pairing of sensational flavor and immense health support for the organs and systems responsible for detoxification.

Ingredients | Yields 1 liter
1 liter water
½ cup blueberries, muddled
1 medium orange, peeled and sliced

1. Prepare a pitcher or water infuser product with 1 liter water.

2. Place the blueberries and orange inside the pitcher or water infuser's canister.

3. Allow mixture to steep in the refrigerator or a cool, dark place for 4–8 hours. For best flavor and health benefits, consume within 24–48 hours.

The Key Ingredients

Blueberries possess a phytochemical, anthocyanin, that not only protects the body and overall health against oxidative stress and toxicity, but also promotes the immune system's healthy functioning. Oranges combine with the blueberries to contribute a sweet, tart flavor sensation that stimulates the senses and pleases the palate while also providing the body with detoxifying benefits that promote healthy functioning.

Dandelion Tea with Ginger and Apple Cider Vinegar

Dandelion greens and teas have a reputation for infusing beverages, smoothies, or foods with a bitter taste. This recipe combines the traditionally bitter dandelion tea with a blend of ginger and apple cider vinegar that not only takes the "bite" out of the infusion but also provides the body with a variety of detoxifying nutrients.

Ingredients | Yields 1 liter

1 liter water
2 dandelion tea bags
2" piece ginger, peeled and sliced
2 tablespoons organic, unfiltered, unpasteurized apple cider vinegar

1. Prepare a pitcher or water infuser product with 1 liter water.

2. Place the tea bags, ginger, and vinegar inside the pitcher or water infuser's canister.

3. Allow mixture to steep in the refrigerator or a cool, dark place for 4–8 hours. For best flavor and health benefits, consume within 24–48 hours.

The Key Ingredients

Delicious detoxification has never tasted better than with this amazing infusion of dandelion tea, spicy ginger, and invigorating apple cider vinegar. Ginger and apple cider vinegar provide an array of phytochemical oils and enzymes, vitamin C, and potent antioxidants. The gingerol and shogaol in ginger combine with the naturally detoxifying and illness-combatting enzymes of apple cider vinegar to protect against the harmful cell degradation and toxicity that can overwhelm the body with free radical damage.

Fig-Cucumber-Melon

The fruity flavors of figs and cantaloupe combine with refreshing cucumber for a water infusion that makes hydration and detoxification not only easy but also delicious!

Ingredients | Yields 1 liter

1 liter water
1 medium fig, peeled and chopped
3" piece cucumber, peeled and sliced
½ cup peeled and chopped cantaloupe

1. Prepare a pitcher or water infuser product with 1 liter water.

2. Place the fig, cucumber, and cantaloupe inside the pitcher or water infuser's canister.

3. Allow mixture to steep in the refrigerator or a cool, dark place for 4–8 hours. For best flavor and health benefits, consume within 24–48 hours.

The Key Ingredients

With potent antioxidants vitamin C, beta-carotene, and vitamin E, the fig, cucumber, and cantaloupe do double duty, providing the body and brain with the essential nutrients they need to thrive, and promoting the healthy functioning of the immune system and the organs involved in natural detoxification processes. With these delicious ingredients' phytochemicals acting to combat toxicity in the blood and throughout the body, the one-two punch of prevention and protection has never tasted better!

Minty Melon-Lime

Not only do these vibrant green ingredients create a drink that is visually appealing and palate-pleasing, but their powerful flavors contribute bountiful benefits to the body and mind, too!

Ingredients | Yields 1 liter
1 liter water
½ cup peeled and chopped honeydew melon
1 large lime, peeled and chopped
⅛ cup chopped mint leaves

1. Prepare a pitcher or water infuser product with 1 liter water.

2. Place the melon, lime, and mint leaves inside the pitcher or water infuser's canister.

3. Allow mixture to steep in the refrigerator or a cool, dark place for 4–8 hours. For best flavor and health benefits, consume within 24–48 hours.

The Key Ingredients

This flavorful blend of ingredients creates a sensational hydration experience that provides the body with all of the essential vitamins, minerals, and antioxidants needed to fend off infection, protect cells against harmful oxidative stress, and promote healthy functioning of the liver and kidneys. With mint's potent phytochemicals that combat bacteria, viruses, and microbes, honeydew's naturally occurring antioxidants, and lime's rich stores of vitamin C, this recipe makes for a delightfully delicious and nutritious way to sip yourself to a cleaner, healthier you!

Chapter 4

Infusions for Improved Immunity

Without a doubt, supporting your immune system is one of the best ways to safeguard your health. Through the provisions of powerful vitamins, minerals, and phytochemicals that act to protect the health of cells, organs, and systems, a clean diet focused on whole foods can help anyone achieve an optimal level of health. Drinking adequate amounts of water daily helps to further support the immune system, ensuring that the body remains hydrated and able to function as intended. Combining nutrient-dense fruits, vegetables, and herbs with your daily doses of water pairs the two most beneficial staples on which the body depends. These delicious infused water recipes can help you enjoy your favorite flavors of fruits, vegetables, and herbs while quenching your thirst, feeling your best, and warding off infections, illness, and disease.

Green Tea with Ginger

The slightly spicy flavor of ginger infuses your water with a delightful bite that works perfectly to balance the natural tang of green tea leaves. This kicked-up creation will keep you healthy and hydrated and give you a little extra pep in your step.

Ingredients | Yields 1 liter

1 liter water
2 organic green tea bags
3 tablespoons peeled and sliced ginger

1. Prepare a pitcher or water infuser product with 1 liter water.

2. Place the green tea bags and sliced ginger inside the pitcher or water infuser's canister.

3. Allow mixture to steep in the refrigerator or a cool, dark place for 8 hours. For best flavor and health benefits, consume within 24–36 hours.

The Key Ingredients

Green tea and spicy ginger make for a powerful combination that supports the immune system with potent antioxidants and a plethora of vitamins and minerals. While ginger adds the compounds shogaol and gingerol to this immunity-boosting recipe, the green tea adds potent catechins that act similarly, protecting the cells and systems against damage and degradation. Green tea also provides an array of naturally occurring phytochemicals and polyphenols that support metabolism, improve immunity, and protect cells against harmful changes caused by free radicals and oxidative stress.

Gingered Grapefruit-Cucumber

Here is a perfectly spiced hydrating treat that not only tastes great but also benefits your immune system, skin, and brain functioning. This delicious combination of vitamin C–rich grapefruit, enzyme-packed ginger, and mineral-filled cucumber makes for an amazing infused water that you can enjoy anytime.

Ingredients | Yields 1 liter

1 liter water
1 small cucumber, peeled and sliced
1 large pink grapefruit, peeled and quartered
3 tablespoons peeled and sliced ginger

1. Prepare a pitcher or water infuser product with 1 liter water.

2. Place cucumber, grapefruit, and ginger inside the pitcher or water infuser's canister.

3. Allow mixture to steep in the refrigerator or a cool, dark place for 4 hours. For best flavor and health benefits, consume within 24–36 hours.

The Key Ingredients

The grapefruit in this recipe provides immunity-boosting nutrients including vitamin C, lycopene, and limonoids (the antioxidant specific to citrus fruits), while the ginger adds its unique antiviral and antibacterial compounds shogaol and gingerol and the cucumber provides silica, selenium, and vitamins A, C, and E. These nutrient-dense ingredients strengthen the body's defense against illness and disease, safeguard the cells and organs against cancerous changes, and improve the body's ability to purge toxins from the bloodstream.

Strawberry-Lime with Mint

Tart lime, sweet strawberries, and refreshing mint fill every sip of this infused water, making for a colorful combination that appeals to the eyes as well as the taste buds. By sipping this colorful concoction throughout your day, you can rehydrate your cells and obtain powerful antioxidants.

Ingredients | Yields 1 liter

1 liter water
6 strawberries, tops removed and sliced
1 large lime, peeled and quartered
2 tablespoons chopped mint leaves

1. Prepare a pitcher or water infuser product with 1 liter water.

2. Place the strawberries, lime, and mint leaves inside the pitcher or water infuser's canister.

3. Allow mixture to steep in the refrigerator or a cool, dark place for 6 hours. For best flavor and health benefits, consume within 24–36 hours.

The Key Ingredients

Rich in vitamins A, C, and E, magnesium, calcium, and a wide variety of potent phytochemicals and polyphenols, this delicious recipe combines strawberries, limes, and mint in a drink that helps safeguard (and improve) the immune system. This water provides cells with protection against damage, disease, and cancerous changes caused by oxidative stress.

Strawberry-Blueberry-Pineapple

With vibrant colors and delicious flavors, the fruits that star in this infused water recipe take hydration to new heights. Simple and sweet, this trio of ingredients makes an immunity-boosting infused water that can be enjoyed any time, anywhere!

Ingredients | Yields 1 liter

1 liter water
5 strawberries, tops removed and sliced
¼ cup blueberries, muddled
1 (¾"-thick) slice of pineapple, peeled and chopped

1. Prepare a pitcher or water infuser product with 1 liter water.

2. Place the strawberries, blueberries, and pineapple inside the pitcher or water infuser's canister.

3. Allow mixture to steep in the refrigerator or a cool, dark place for 4–8 hours. For best flavor and health benefits, consume within 24–48 hours.

The Key Ingredients

Bright red strawberries, rich in the potent phytochemical anthocyanins, combine with blueberries' natural stores of antioxidant anthocyanadins to support the immune system, safeguard the respiratory system against illness and disease, and combat free radical damage within the cells. Add to these benefits the beautiful bromelain- and beta-carotene-packed pineapple, and you've got a sensational recipe that not only protects the body against illness and disease by promoting the immune system's functioning, but also tastes absolutely amazing!

Lemon-Oregano

This flavorful duo combines to create a savory, hydrating concoction that promotes the health and well-being of the entire body! The citrusy goodness of lemons combines with oregano for a taste sensation that makes every drop of this infused water recipe truly delicious.

Ingredients | Yields 1 liter

1 liter water
¼ cup whole oregano leaves
2 large lemons, peeled and sliced

1. Prepare a pitcher or water infuser product with 1 liter water.

2. Place the oregano leaves and lemons inside the pitcher or water infuser's canister.

3. Allow mixture to steep in the refrigerator or a cool, dark place for 4–8 hours. For best flavor and health benefits, consume within 24–48 hours.

The Key Ingredients

With potent doses of vitamin C that strengthen and support the immune system, both lemons and oregano infuse their delicious flavors and spectacular nutrition to create a health-boosting combination that goes above and beyond. This drink contains potent phytochemicals, including lemons' limonins and oregano's carvacrol and thymol, that act as potent antibacterial, antiviral, and antimicrobial agents to protect against cold and flu while preventing free radical damage within the cells.

Strawberry-Kiwi-Melon

This infused water recipe uses a blend of vibrant, sweet fruits that infuse the water with amazing flavor, powerful nutrition, and effective immune system support that can help you safeguard your health with every delicious sip.

Ingredients | Yields 1 liter

1 liter water
6 strawberries, tops removed and sliced
1 medium kiwi, peeled and diced
¼ cup peeled and chopped honeydew melon

1. Prepare a pitcher or water infuser product with 1 liter water.

2. Place the strawberries, kiwi, and honeydew inside the pitcher or water infuser's canister.

3. Allow mixture to steep in the refrigerator or a cool, dark place for 4–8 hours. For best flavor and health benefits, consume within 24–48 hours.

The Key Ingredients

Sweet strawberries join forces with delicious kiwifruit and subtle honeydew to provide an incredible amount of vitamin C, antioxidants, and anti-inflammatory compounds that combine to protect the cells and systems against illness and disease. With antimicrobial, antibacterial, and antiviral benefits, the potent doses of vitamin C in these fruits ensure that your cells remain free of free radical damage and your immune system functions as intended.

Blackberry-Apple

Few people are aware of the astounding amount of nutrition that comes packed in every blackberry. The unassuming blackberry contains phytochemicals that the immune system needs in order to remain fully functioning and fully protected!

Ingredients | Yields 1 liter

1 liter water
½ cup blackberries, muddled
1 medium apple, peeled, cored, and chopped

1. Prepare a pitcher or water infuser product with 1 liter water.

2. Place the blackberries and apple inside the pitcher or water infuser's canister.

3. Allow mixture to steep in the refrigerator or a cool, dark place for 4–8 hours. For best flavor and health benefits, consume within 24–48 hours.

The Key Ingredients

The blackberries contain phytochemicals called anthocyanadins that give this berry its deep purple shade. These phytochemicals act as powerful antioxidants and anti-inflammatory compounds, seeking out free radicals and pro-inflammatory proteins that can wreak havoc on the body. The apple also contributes to the health-boosting nutrition of this recipe. Vitamin C, quercetin, and magnesium from the apple round out this delicious blend of ingredients with the vitamins, minerals, and naturally occurring phytochemicals your immune system needs.

Berry-Lemon

The variety of vitamins, minerals, and phytochemicals in this delicious blend of sweet and tart ingredients is nothing short of impressive. Helping you stay healthy with every last sip, this recipe's ingredients make living better easy!

Ingredients | Yields 1 liter

1 liter water
½ cup blueberries, muddled
5 strawberries, tops removed and sliced
½ large lemon, peeled and sliced

1. Prepare a pitcher or water infuser product with 1 liter water.

2. Place the berries and lemon slices inside the pitcher or water infuser's canister.

3. Allow mixture to steep in the refrigerator or a cool, dark place for 4–8 hours. For best flavor and health benefits, consume within 24–48 hours.

The Key Ingredients

If your goal is to improve immunity, naturally detoxify, boost brain functioning, or safeguard cells against harmful changes that result from free radical damage and oxidative stress, this blend of berries and citrus is the perfect prescription. Providing B vitamins, vitamins A, C, E, and K, potassium, magnesium, calcium, and iron, as well as anthocyanins of the strawberries, anthocyanadins of the blueberries, and limonins of the lemons, these fruits make a fantastic feast for the body's natural processes involved in immunity.

Lemon-Lime-Basil

Gorgeous yellow lemons combine with vibrant green limes and basil leaves for a visually pleasing taste sensation that not only tickles your taste buds, but provides the entire body with protective and preventative nutrition.

Ingredients | Yields 1 liter
1 liter water
½ large lemon, peeled and sliced
½ large lime, peeled and sliced
¼ cup basil leaves, chopped

1. Prepare a pitcher or water infuser product with 1 liter water.
2. Place the lemon, lime, and basil inside the pitcher or water infuser's canister.
3. Allow mixture to steep in the refrigerator or a cool, dark place for 4–8 hours. For best flavor and health benefits, consume within 24–48 hours.

The Key Ingredients

Vitamin C does double duty in this recipe, acting both as an essential vitamin needed by the immune system to fight off illness effectively and as a powerful antioxidant that fends off free radical damage within the cells. The addition of basil provides a variety of phytochemicals that help to cleanse the blood and body of toxins that can wreak havoc on the liver. By supporting liver health, protecting the cells, and boosting the immune system, this drink makes for a tasty treat that ensures you stay healthy.

Green Tea with Ginger and Apple Cider Vinegar

With delicious flavors that perfectly complement one another, this infused water recipe's ingredients make for a great combination of nutrient-dense hydration that keeps you healthy and strong!

Ingredients | Yields 1 liter
1 liter water
2 organic green tea bags
1" piece ginger, peeled and sliced
1 tablespoon organic, unfiltered, unpasteurized apple cider vinegar

1. Prepare a pitcher or water infuser product with 1 liter water.

2. Place the green tea bags, ginger, and vinegar inside the pitcher or water infuser's canister.

3. Allow mixture to steep in the refrigerator or a cool, dark place for 4–8 hours. For best flavor and health benefits, consume within 24–48 hours.

The Key Ingredients

The potency of green tea's antioxidants and catechins joins forces with the naturally occurring enzymes and oils of ginger and apple cider vinegar to produce an infused water experience that goes above and beyond the benefits of any other tea tonic. Packed with plentiful antioxidants that support the cells' health while safeguarding the immune system against illness and disease, vitamin C and phytochemicals help to prevent the infiltration of microbes, bacteria, and viruses that can wreak havoc on the body.

Ginger-Pear

The spice of ginger adds to the subtle sweetness of pears, creating an infused water recipe that takes each sip of your daily doses of hydration to new heights. This sweet and spicy mix makes for a delicious way to achieve better health naturally.

Ingredients | Yields 1 liter
1 liter water
1" piece ginger, peeled and sliced
2 medium pears, peeled, cored, and chopped

1. Prepare a pitcher or water infuser product with 1 liter water.

2. Place the ginger and pears inside the pitcher or water infuser's canister.

3. Allow mixture to steep in the refrigerator or a cool, dark place for 4–8 hours. For best flavor and health benefits, consume within 24–48 hours.

The Key Ingredients

Pears and ginger combine to create an immunity-boosting blend of nutrition that can help safeguard your health. This recipe is packed with B vitamins, vitamins A, C, and E, and minerals including calcium, magnesium, and zinc, as well as a variety of potent antioxidants. Helping to protect the body against infections of all kinds, the ginger helps fight microbes, bacteria, and viruses, while pears contribute their unique phytochemical, quercetin, which helps regulate the health and well-being of the gut.

Cinnamon-Apple

The delicious sweetness of apples combines with the unique essence of cinnamon in this sweet treat that not only tastes great but also provides the body with bountiful benefits. All of these ingredients work beautifully together to please the palate and keep you healthy, too!

Ingredients | Yields 1 liter

1 liter water
2 medium Granny Smith apples, peeled, cored, and chopped
2 cinnamon sticks
1 tablespoon organic, unfiltered, unpasteurized apple cider vinegar

1. Prepare a pitcher or water infuser product with 1 liter water.

2. Place the apples, cinnamon, and vinegar inside the pitcher or water infuser's canister.

3. Allow mixture to steep in the refrigerator or a cool, dark place for 4–8 hours. For best flavor and health benefits, consume within 24–48 hours.

The Key Ingredients

Combining these three simple ingredients creates a plethora of potent phytochemicals that improve everything from cell health to blood clarity. Vitamins A, C, and E act as effective antioxidants, helping to support the cellular structures and maintain cell health. Fighting off microbial, bacterial, and viral infections, cinnamon's blend of phytochemicals makes it easier for the immune system to function as intended. Finally, the slightly tart addition of apple cider vinegar cleanses the blood and gut of toxins and impurities with its naturally occurring enzymes.

Chapter 5

Infusions for Healthy Skin and Anti-Aging

Consumers spend billions of dollars every year on cleansers, creams, and treatments that promise to provide beautiful skin, but few (if any!) actually deliver the results. The reason is simple: Healthy skin starts on the inside. Wrinkles, blemishes, discoloration, and skin issues arise from imbalances and inadequate supplies of nutrients within the body. When the body's stores of nutrients are depleted, or overwhelming amounts of toxins are absorbed from the environment or consumed in the diet, the results are displayed on the skin. Every pore and every inch of the skin portrays the internal health of the body. So if beautiful skin is what you seek, infused water can help! Because a startling majority of people do not consume the daily recommended amount of water, it's no wonder that skin-care issues are a major concern. The inadequate hydration starves the skin of the nutrition it needs and contributes to troublesome skin conditions. With delicious, refreshing combinations of vibrant fruits, vegetables, and herbs that provide the body and skin with powerful vitamins, minerals, and phytochemicals, these infused water recipes hydrate the body's cells while promoting and protecting the health of the entire body, helping you to achieve beautiful skin that radiates health from the inside out!

Very Berry Apple

Why waste your time and money on products that promise healthy skin, but seldom work, when you could enjoy a delicious hydrating experience like that provided by this infused water recipe?

Ingredients | Yields 1 liter

1 liter water
¼ cup raspberries, muddled
¼ cup blueberries, muddled
1 medium Fuji apple, peeled, cored, and chopped

1. Prepare a pitcher or water infuser product with 1 liter water.

2. Place the raspberries, blueberries, and apple inside the pitcher or water infuser's canister.

3. Allow mixture to steep in the refrigerator or a cool, dark place for 4–8 hours. For best flavor and health benefits, consume within 24–48 hours.

The Key Ingredients

The ingredients in this recipe are packed with phytochemicals that provide the body and skin with restorative vitamins including vitamin C, minerals including calcium, potassium, and zinc, and an abundance of antioxidants. These antioxidants help fight free radical damage that can wreak havoc on the cells and degrade the components of the skin that give you a youthful appearance. Promoting the health and well-being of the skin's cells and elastin and collagen proteins, this recipe's ingredients make for a delicious way to sip your skin healthier!

Purple Pomegranate

This recipe's beautiful blend of berries, pomegranate, and grapes provides superior skin protection while supporting the body's overall health and well-being.

Ingredients | Yields 1 liter

1 liter water
½ cup blackberries, muddled
½ cup pomegranate jewels, muddled
4 purple grapes, halved

1. Prepare a pitcher or water infuser product with 1 liter water.

2. Place the blackberries, pomegranate jewels, and grapes inside the pitcher or water infuser's canister.

3. Allow mixture to steep in the refrigerator or a cool, dark place for 4–8 hours. For best flavor and health benefits, consume within 24–48 hours.

The Key Ingredients

This infused water recipe delivers great taste with a wide variety of benefits to the brain and body. Vitamins A, C, and E ensure proper functioning of the body's processes and act as potent protective antioxidants. This is a beautifying brain-boosting combination that maintains optimal cell health and functioning; protects against free radical damage that can degrade cell health and lead to harmful illnesses and chronic conditions; and promotes the health of the skin, eyes, hair, and nails.

Kiwi-Watermelon

The tremendous taste of kiwi infuses every last drop of this delicious recipe, pairing up with watermelon to make for a refreshing dose of hydration loaded with nutrients and immense benefits to both body and mind.

Ingredients | Yields 1 liter

1 liter water
1 medium kiwi, peeled and sliced
1 cup peeled and chopped watermelon

1. Prepare a pitcher or water infuser product with 1 liter water.

2. Place the kiwi and watermelon inside the pitcher or water infuser's canister.

3. Allow mixture to steep in the refrigerator or a cool, dark place for 4–8 hours. For best flavor and health benefits, consume within 24–48 hours.

The Key Ingredients

Helping to replenish lost stores of nutrients including vitamin C, magnesium, and zinc, these fruits combine to ensure that the body has these essential nutrients available, and also improve the body's ability to store and process them. This recipe is a delightful blend of fun fruits that support the healthy cells of the brain, fight toxicity and cellular degradation, and maintain proper functioning of the immune system, nervous system, and detoxification process.

Mango-Grape

Mango's beautiful yellow-orange hue signifies the intense nutrition that infuses every ounce of this delightful recipe.

Ingredients | Yields 1 liter

1 liter water
½ cup peeled and chopped mango
¼ cup halved red grapes
¼ cup halved green grapes

1. Prepare a pitcher or water infuser product with 1 liter water.

2. Place the mango and grapes inside the pitcher or water infuser's canister.

3. Allow mixture to steep in the refrigerator or a cool, dark place for 4–8 hours. For best flavor and health benefits, consume within 24–48 hours.

The Key Ingredients

Mango's potent beta-carotene helps the body fight inflammation inside and out by combating the processes caused by pro-inflammatory compounds that can destroy cell health and create chronic conditions, such as arthritis. With the addition of resveratrol-rich grapes, this infusion also protects the skin, hair, and nails from harmful changes by safeguarding the cells and nutrient-delivery processes, ensuring that your outside looks just as healthy and young as the inside!

Grape-Grapefruit

Grapes and grapefruit combine in this sweet and slightly tart recipe to provide the body and brain with intense health benefits that can only be achieved with proper nutrition.

Ingredients | Yields 1 liter
1 liter water
½ cup red grapes, halved
½ large white grapefruit, peeled and sliced

1. Prepare a pitcher or water infuser product with 1 liter water.

2. Place the grapes and grapefruit inside the pitcher or water infuser's canister.

3. Allow mixture to steep in the refrigerator or a cool, dark place for 4–8 hours. For best flavor and health benefits, consume within 24–48 hours.

The Key Ingredients

The consumption of adequate vitamin C along with vitamins A and E make protecting the body's health while promoting a youthful appearance easier than ever! These potent antioxidants act alongside the grapes' phytonutrient, resveratrol, to preserve the health of skin cells and the collagen and elastin that can weaken and deteriorate with age, leading to blemishes, discoloration, wrinkles, and sagging. Sipping a sweet, citrusy blend like this one can help you to support your systems, improve immunity, and preserve your skin's health.

Perfect Papaya-Grape

The anti-aging benefits of this fruit infusion promote the health of a particular area of the body that can be severely affected as we age: the eyes. With plentiful doses of beta-carotene in the papaya, the body is able to generate vitamin A, and use this essential vitamin to support the health and well-being of the eyes.

Ingredients | Yields 1 liter
1 liter water
⅔ cup Concord grapes, halved
⅔ cup peeled and chopped papaya

1. Prepare a pitcher or water infuser product with 1 liter water.
2. Place the grapes and papaya inside the pitcher or water infuser's canister.
3. Allow mixture to steep in the refrigerator or a cool, dark place for 4–8 hours. For best flavor and health benefits, consume within 24–48 hours.

The Key Ingredients

The risk of macular degeneration increases as we age, and papaya's natural stores of nutrients combat the inflammation, degradation, and oxidative stress on the eye's cells and structures, helping to improve and maintain eye health. With the grape's healthy doses of potent anthocyanins that act to combat free radicals and toxins, this blend gets even brighter for the eyes by helping to maintain adequate oxygen and nutrient delivery of all of the essentials needed for healthy eyes.

Blueberry-Mango

When beautiful blueberries combine with the exquisite nectar of mango, the feast for the eyes is also a perfect promoter of brain health. Better brain functioning with every sip of this infusion makes for a deliciously hydrating way to achieve great health!

Ingredients | Yields 1 liter

1 liter water
⅔ cup blueberries, muddled
½ cup peeled and sliced mango

1. Prepare a pitcher or water infuser product with 1 liter water.

2. Place the blueberries and mango inside the pitcher or water infuser's canister.

3. Allow mixture to steep in the refrigerator or a cool, dark place for 4–8 hours. For best flavor and health benefits, consume within 24–48 hours.

The Key Ingredients

With age, the systems that directly affect the health of the brain can suffer from toxicity, illness, inflammation, and chronic conditions that can lead to disease. With this blend of berries and mango, the B vitamins and potent minerals such as calcium and magnesium combine with powerful antioxidants to protect the blood, body, and brain from harmful toxicity; support the communication between the nerves and brain; and maintain a healthy cardiovascular system to ensure optimal oxygen delivery.

Kiwi-Melon

Vibrant kiwis combine with the light green lusciousness of honeydew for a flavor combination that's a delicious way to deliver maximum nutrition to the entire body. With top-notch protection against inflammation that can wreak havoc on the health, this mix of kiwi and melon is the simplest way to achieve optimal health sweetly.

Ingredients | Yields 1 liter

1 liter water
1 medium kiwi, peeled and sliced
½ cup peeled and chopped honeydew melon

1. Prepare a pitcher or water infuser product with 1 liter water.

2. Place the kiwi and melon inside the pitcher or water infuser's canister.

3. Allow mixture to steep in the refrigerator or a cool, dark place for 4–8 hours. For best flavor and health benefits, consume within 24–48 hours.

The Key Ingredients

With rich stores of vitamins A, C, and E, along with minerals including silica, calcium, and magnesium, plus phytochemicals that provide antioxidant protection, this delicious and nutritious infusion gives the body everything it needs to stay healthy, happy, and as vibrant as the colors of these delectable ingredients. Pleasing the palate while hydrating the cells, this recipe also makes for a healthy mix of anti-inflammatory compounds that fight inflammation deep in the cells, within the joints, and throughout the skin.

Papaya-Citrus with Grape

Delicious and nutritious, this citrusy sweet blend of beautiful fruits colors your daily doses of water with nutrition you can see and feel!

Ingredients | Yields 1 liter
1 liter water
½ cup peeled and sliced papaya
½ large pink grapefruit, peeled and sliced
½ cup halved Concord grapes

1. Prepare a pitcher or water infuser product with 1 liter water.

2. Place the papaya, grapefruit, and grapes inside the pitcher or water infuser's canister.

3. Allow mixture to steep in the refrigerator or a cool, dark place for 4–8 hours. For best flavor and health benefits, consume within 24–48 hours.

The Key Ingredients

With citrusy sweetness, grapefruits pack vital amounts of vitamin C into every scrumptious sip of this infusion, helping to provide the body with powerful protection against free radical damage and oxidative stress that can degrade cell health of the organs. Further supporting the cellular health of the body's organs and systems, the natural nutrients and antioxidants in papaya and grapes directly affect and protect everything from eye health and bone health to the proper processing and storage of nutrients needed to maintain muscle mass and even retain memory.

Pear-Apple-Grape

The subtle sweetness of pears and apples combines with the unique taste of red grapes for an inspirational infusion that will keep your skin looking better than ever.

Ingredients | Yields 1 liter

1 liter water
½ medium pear, peeled, cored, and sliced
½ medium apple, peeled, cored, and sliced
½ cup halved red grapes

1. Prepare a pitcher or water infuser product with 1 liter water.
2. Place the pear, apple, and grapes inside the pitcher or water infuser's canister.
3. Allow mixture to steep in the refrigerator or a cool, dark place for 4–8 hours. For best flavor and health benefits, consume within 24–48 hours.

The Key Ingredients

Cleansing the blood and body of impurities, these ingredients provide B vitamins and potent antioxidants that not only support detoxification naturally, but also keep the liver and kidneys functioning as well as possible. Further supporting skin health are antioxidants such as resveratrol, which not only safeguard cell health but directly support the body's regeneration of skin cells and the healthy production of collagen and elastin, all of which help to fend off wrinkles and keep skin supple.

Grape-Kiwi-Nectarine

Sweet, juicy, and with a variety of colors as different as the nutrients they provide, the ingredients in this infused water recipe ensure that your needs are met when it comes to nutrition.

Ingredients | Yields 1 liter

1 liter water
½ cup halved Concord grapes
1 medium kiwi, peeled and sliced
1 medium nectarine, peeled, pitted, and sliced

1. Prepare a pitcher or water infuser product with 1 liter water.

2. Place the grapes, kiwi, and nectarine inside the pitcher or water infuser's canister.

3. Allow mixture to steep in the refrigerator or a cool, dark place for 4–8 hours. For best flavor and health benefits, consume within 24–48 hours.

The Key Ingredients

The grapes' resveratrol, nectarine's beta-carotene, and kiwifruit's healthy doses of vitamin C give your skin a boost as these restorative antioxidants work hard to maintain proper cell structure and health, and minimize decline or degradation in the strength of the skin's elasticity and suppleness. Calcium, potassium, and magnesium from each of these fruits improve brain health. This concoction helps to preserve the abilities of the brain by protecting the cells, promoting cognitive processes, and supporting nervous system communication between the brain and the body.

Green Tea with Apples and Grapes

Delicious flavors of apples and grapes help to infuse a subtle sweetness into the traditionally slightly bitter-tasting green tea in this recipe.

Ingredients | Yields 1 liter

1 liter water
2 organic green tea bags
1 medium apple, peeled, cored, and sliced
1 cup halved Concord grapes

1. Prepare a pitcher or water infuser product with 1 liter water.

2. Place the tea bags, apple, and grapes inside the pitcher or water infuser's canister.

3. Allow mixture to steep in the refrigerator or a cool, dark place for 4–8 hours. For best flavor and health benefits, consume within 24–48 hours.

The Key Ingredients

This recipe's ingredients work well together to ensure that the body gets a variety of necessary nutrients, and in the natural state in which they are the most effective. Apples' unique quercetin, grapes' resveratrol, and green tea's catechins added to B vitamins, vitamins A, C, E, and K, and magnesium, calcium, iron, and potassium provide an army of potent antioxidants that fight free radicals.

Great Grape-Citrus

This fruit-infused water recipe contributes benefits galore, with each nutrient working together to improve and safeguard the health and functioning of the cells, organs, and systems throughout the body, and helping you maintain health and beauty throughout your years.

Ingredients | Yields 1 liter
1 liter water
1 medium red grapefruit, peeled and sliced
1 small tangerine, peeled and sliced
¾ cup red grapes, halved

1. Prepare a pitcher or water infuser product with 1 liter water.

2. Place the grapefruit, tangerine, and grapes inside the pitcher or water infuser's canister.

3. Allow mixture to steep in the refrigerator or a cool, dark place for 4–8 hours. For best flavor and health benefits, consume within 24–48 hours.

The Key Ingredients

With the vitamin C supporting immunity, B vitamins boosting brain functioning, and minerals such as calcium, magnesium, and potassium ensuring that bone strength, muscle mass maintenance, and proper nervous system functioning remain top notch, the combination of grapefruit, tangerine, and grapes not only tastes amazing but has amazing benefits for your health.

Chapter 6

Infusions for Weight Loss

Weight loss is an area of focus for a large majority of people around the world. Whether the goal is to lose five pounds or fifty, efforts to lose weight can be challenging. Because of the numerous factors that contribute to weight gain—such as genetics, level of health, and lifestyle choices—few people are able to achieve and maintain their goal weight easily and consistently throughout their lifetime. While pills, potions, and programs promise to deliver weight-loss success, the most effective way to lose weight and maintain weight loss is to focus on the daily diet and lifestyle habits that help the body's functions that directly correlate to weight. With a diet focused on clean, whole foods, the body is able to absorb the nutrients it needs, support the systems involved with metabolic processes, and increase energy to further support weight-loss efforts such as exercise and activity. The additions of nutritious fruits, vegetables, and herbs to your daily doses of drinking water make for flavorful hydration that's infused with the essential nutrients the body needs to thrive. Vitamins, minerals, and phytochemicals ensure that the body has adequate supplies of the nutrients it needs for simple weight loss, helping you to experience weight-loss success healthfully!

Strawberry-Basil

Basil and strawberry team up in this metabolism-boosting fruit-and-herb-infused water recipe to maximize weight loss in a number of ways.

Ingredients | Yields 1 liter

1 liter water
10 strawberries, tops removed and sliced
¼ cup basil leaves, chopped

1. Prepare a pitcher or water infuser product with 1 liter water.

2. Place the strawberries and basil inside the pitcher or water infuser's canister.

3. Allow mixture to steep in the refrigerator or a cool, dark place for 4–8 hours. For best flavor and health benefits, consume within 24–48 hours.

The Key Ingredients

Through their rich provisions of essential nutrients including the B vitamins and vitamins A, C, E, and K, basil and strawberries not only support the proper absorption of essential minerals such as iron and calcium but also support the immune system, boost energy levels, and help maintain proper metabolic functions that improve weight loss. Add to those vitamins the healthy doses of iron, copper, magnesium, and calcium found in this drink, and you've got a prescription for improved protein synthesis that helps the body lose fat, build muscle, and have more energy.

Tropical Cherry-Apple

Brimming with delicious flavors and vibrant colors, this trio of fruits combines to create an infused water recipe that not only keeps you hydrated but provides your body and brain with essential vitamins, minerals, and protective antioxidants that help you lose weight naturally.

Ingredients | Yields 1 liter

1 liter water
¼ cup pitted cherries, chopped
1 (¼"-thick) slice of pineapple, peeled and chopped
1 small apple, cored and sliced

1. Prepare a pitcher or water infuser product with 1 liter water.

2. Place the cherries, pineapple, and apple inside the pitcher or water infuser's canister.

3. Allow mixture to steep in the refrigerator or a cool, dark place for 4–8 hours. For best flavor and health benefits, consume within 24–48 hours.

The Key Ingredients

Some of the most essential nutrients needed by the body are those that calm cravings and regulate blood sugar, blood pressure, and hormone production. With rich stores of iron, calcium, and magnesium, the cherries, pineapple, and apple in this recipe provide the body with this necessary nutrition, keeping your energy levels high while calming cravings and ensuring that hormones stay at the perfect levels to promote weight loss. Add to these benefits the potent antioxidants that support cell health and you've got a delicious recipe for better health and weight-loss success!

Spicy Cucumber

Slightly spicy, yet cool as a cucumber, this delightful hydration creation with a kick may be the perfect pairing for your weight-loss goals, helping you to achieve optimal health and a desirable weight!

Ingredients | Yields 1 liter

1 liter water
1 medium jalapeño pepper, deseeded and sliced
1 medium cucumber, peeled and sliced

1. Prepare a pitcher or water infuser product with 1 liter water.

2. Place the jalapeño and cucumber inside the pitcher or water infuser's canister.

3. Allow mixture to steep in the refrigerator or a cool, dark place for 4–8 hours. For best flavor and health benefits, consume within 24–48 hours.

The Key Ingredients

Revving up the metabolism with the spicy addition of jalapeño, this infused water recipe provides a generous dose of capsaicin, a naturally occurring phytochemical in jalapeños that gives it its special kick. In the body, capsaicin has a natural warming effect that stimulates the metabolic processes involved with burning fat. Vitamin C from both the jalapeño and cucumber takes this benefit even further by improving the body's ability to absorb the essential minerals, calcium and iron, that are required in the processes of protein synthesis, muscle maintenance, and bone health.

Grape-Melon

This drink provides vitamins, minerals, and potent antioxidants that combine to deliver what your body needs to stay focused and energized and to improve your fat-burning potential. But that's not all; you also get the benefit of improved immunity, better blood health, and even skin health benefits!

Ingredients | Yields 1 liter
1 liter water
½ cup halved red grapes
½ cup peeled and chopped honeydew melon

1. Prepare a pitcher or water infuser product with 1 liter water.

2. Place the grapes and honeydew inside the pitcher or water infuser's canister.

3. Allow mixture to steep in the refrigerator or a cool, dark place for 4–8 hours. For best flavor and health benefits, consume within 24–48 hours.

The Key Ingredients

Every sip of this infusion delivers powerful provisions of the precise nutrients needed to fight fatigue, improve energy levels, and maintain energy and focus throughout the day. B vitamins, vitamin C, and vitamin K combine with rich stores of iron, calcium, and potassium to help support the body's metabolism, improve protein synthesis, and regulate hormones and brain chemicals, such as serotonin and dopamine, that directly affect energy and mood. With the added benefit of regulated blood sugar levels and blood pressure, you can also enjoy a day with fewer cravings.

Pineapple-Grape

Helping to improve your blood health, this recipe's delightful blend of bromelain-packed pineapple and resveratrol-rich grapes is a delicious way to achieve optimal overall health while also improving the look and health of the skin.

Ingredients | Yields 1 liter
1 liter water
½ cup peeled and chopped pineapple
½ cup red grapes, halved

1. Prepare a pitcher or water infuser product with 1 liter water.

2. Place pineapple and grapes inside the pitcher or water infuser's canister.

3. Allow mixture to steep in the refrigerator or a cool, dark place for 4–8 hours. For best flavor and health benefits, consume within 24–48 hours.

The Key Ingredients

Blood health is a critical factor in fat loss, muscle maintenance, and balanced hormone production. Responsible for the delivery of oxygen to the body, brain, and all organs and systems, the blood and cardiovascular system require vitamins, minerals, and protective antioxidants in order to remain healthy. Pineapple and grapes provide the body with B vitamins, vitamins C, A, and E, and minerals including iron, potassium, and magnesium, all of which support the cardiovascular system's functioning and improve the blood's ability to carry oxygen to the brain and through the body. Adding to these nutrients are grapes' resveratrol and pineapple's bromelain, which act as natural antioxidants, protecting the blood cells from degradation and scavenging the blood of toxins and dead or damaged cells.

Purple Cantaloupe

The average estimate is that diet controls about 70 percent of weight loss, so if you're not delivering the nutrients your body needs to build muscle, burn fat, and increase metabolism, those hours in the gym aren't nearly as effective as they could be with optimal nutrition.

Ingredients | Yields 1 liter
1 liter water
½ cup Concord grapes, halved
½ cup peeled and chopped cantaloupe

1. Prepare a pitcher or water infuser product with 1 liter water.

2. Place the grapes and cantaloupe inside the pitcher or water infuser's canister.

3. Allow mixture to steep in the refrigerator or a cool, dark place for 4–8 hours. For best flavor and health benefits, consume within 24–48 hours.

The Key Ingredients

This simple blend of fruit-infused water uses deep purple Concord grapes and vibrant cantaloupe to provide the body with a variety of nutrients that maximize the functioning of the muscles, digestive system, cardiovascular system, and brain to allow every intricate part of the process of weight loss to function at its full potential. This recipe also contains B vitamins and vitamins C, E, and K, along with minerals calcium and iron, anthocyanins, and beta-carotene.

Green Trio

This delightful trio of green fruits makes for the perfect pairing of delicious flavors and nutrients that can help you sip yourself skinny. Potent antioxidants sweep through this infusion, helping you to maintain the proper metabolic health, healthy bone density, and muscle mass maintenance that support the healthy burning of fat.

Ingredients | Yields 1 liter

1 liter water
¼ cup halved green grapes
1 medium kiwi, peeled and sliced
½ cup peeled and chopped honeydew melon

1. Prepare a pitcher or water infuser product with 1 liter water.

2. Place grapes, kiwi, and honeydew inside the pitcher or water infuser's canister.

3. Allow mixture to steep in the refrigerator or a cool, dark place for 4–8 hours. For best flavor and health benefits, consume within 24–48 hours.

The Key Ingredients

Containing potent antioxidants, each fruit contributes a massive amount of nutrition that helps heal and restore cells, organs, and systems to ensure that your body remains healthy. With B vitamins, vitamin C, and an assortment of minerals and antioxidants that promote proper brain functioning, you have more energy, less hormone fluctuation, and better blood flow to the muscles and organs involved in activity and metabolism. With improved immunity, you safeguard yourself against illness and disease that can wreak havoc on your health (and your ability to engage in exercise!).

Prickly Pear

Ginger comes to the rescue of stalled weight loss with its delicious and nutritious additions to this delightful infused water recipe. The pairing of pear and ginger makes for a sweet, spicy hydration experience that benefits body and mind while you succeed at your weight-loss goals.

Ingredients | Yields 1 liter

1 liter water
2 medium pears, peeled, cored and sliced
1" piece ginger, peeled and sliced

1. Prepare a pitcher or water infuser product with 1 liter water.

2. Place pears and ginger inside the pitcher or water infuser's canister.

3. Allow mixture to steep in the refrigerator or a cool, dark place for 4–8 hours. For best flavor and health benefits, consume within 24–48 hours.

The Key Ingredients

Providing rich polyphenols in its compounds gingerol and shogaol, ginger's slight spiciness not only provides the body with fat-burning enzymes, but also brings an astounding array of nutrients that target the blood's toxins, restore the gut's healthy balance of good bacteria, and promote proper hormone production. Pears further support these aspects of health with vitamin C, calcium, and potassium, ensuring ample amounts of essential nutrients to process and store vitamins and minerals, reduce the belly fat that accumulates due to imbalanced hormones, and invigorate the body and mind for improved energy.

Spiced Watermelon

The unique flavor of sweet watermelon gets spiced up with the addition of ginger in this delicious recipe that gets your body and mind moving!

Ingredients | Yields 1 liter

1 liter water
1 cup peeled and chopped watermelon
1" piece ginger, peeled and sliced

1. Prepare a pitcher or water infuser product with 1 liter water.

2. Place watermelon and ginger inside the pitcher or water infuser's canister.

3. Allow mixture to steep in the refrigerator or a cool, dark place for 4–8 hours. For best flavor and health benefits, consume within 24–48 hours.

The Key Ingredients

Ginger's unique compounds gingerol and shogaol improve blood flow, helping your brain and muscles receive oxygen for improved performance. Watermelon delivers iron, calcium, and protein for ample provisions of muscle-strengthening nutrients that help not only with muscle mass maintenance and performance, but also with repair of muscle cells after your workout. This recipe also provides cell-protecting antioxidants to ensure that cells within the blood, body, and brain remain healthy and able to function as needed in energy production, cognitive processes, and activity.

Citrus Burst

An invigorating blend of citrus fruits and tropical pineapple infuses every drop of your daily doses of hydration with potent vitamins, minerals, and phytochemicals that stimulate the brain naturally, helping to maintain optimal levels of hormones, increase metabolic functioning, and maintain high energy levels throughout the day.

Ingredients | Yields 1 liter

1 liter water
1 medium tangerine, peeled and sliced
1 ($\frac{1}{4}$"-thick) slice of pineapple, peeled and chopped
$\frac{1}{2}$ medium white grapefruit, peeled and sliced

1. Prepare a pitcher or water infuser product with 1 liter water.

2. Place the tangerine, pineapple, and grapefruit inside the pitcher or water infuser's canister.

3. Allow mixture to steep in the refrigerator or a cool, dark place for 4–8 hours. For best flavor and health benefits, consume within 24–48 hours.

The Key Ingredients

This infusion allows you to enjoy all of the flavors and benefits of citrus without the drawbacks of blood sugar spikes, impaired mental functioning, and toxicity that can result from the sweeteners and additives found in store-bought juices. Help your brain become rejuvenated and nourished with the B vitamins, vitamins A and C, and magnesium and calcium in this mix. You can start your day the healthy way with infused water that packs protective antioxidants along with essential nutrients from fruits that taste great!

Very Berry Cherry

This infusion is a refreshing hydration experience that can kick-start your day or jump-start your mid-afternoon slump. This beautiful blend of strawberries, blueberries, raspberries, and cherries helps give your metabolic system the protection and high performance it needs to help you lose weight.

Ingredients | Yields 1 liter
1 liter water
4 strawberries, tops removed and sliced
¼ cup blueberries, muddled
¼ cup raspberries, muddled
½ cup pitted cherries, muddled

1. Prepare a pitcher or water infuser product with 1 liter water.

2. Place the strawberries, blueberries, raspberries, and cherries inside the pitcher or water infuser's canister.

3. Allow mixture to steep in the refrigerator or a cool, dark place for 4–8 hours. For best flavor and health benefits, consume within 24–48 hours.

The Key Ingredients

These ingredients provide powerful nutrients—B vitamins that better the brain's functioning, vitamin C that stimulates your senses while boosting your immunity, and minerals that help support the body's natural processing and use of nutrients. With antioxidants and polyphenols including anthocyanins and anthocyanadins, these berries and cherries maximize the functioning of hormonal processes, balance blood pressure, minimize blood sugar spikes, and ensure that detoxification of the blood, body, and brain remains top-notch, so you can enjoy more energy, less toxicity, and better focus with every sip.

Spicy Citrus

The sweetness of kiwifruit, the slightly tart citrus, and the spiciness of ginger come together in this fruit-infused flavor sensation that hydrates the cells, body, and brain while delivering powerful nutrition to every system involved in weight-loss success.

Ingredients | Yields 1 liter

1 liter water
½ medium pink grapefruit, peeled and sliced
1 medium kiwi, peeled and sliced
1" piece ginger, peeled and sliced

1. Prepare a pitcher or water infuser product with 1 liter water.

2. Place the grapefruit, kiwi, and ginger inside the pitcher or water infuser's canister.

3. Allow mixture to steep in the refrigerator or a cool, dark place for 4–8 hours. For best flavor and health benefits, consume within 24–48 hours.

The Key Ingredients

The antioxidants, polyphenols, oils, and compounds gingerol and shogaol that infuse this recipe help you achieve the energy, focus, and fast metabolism you need to lose weight. In this drink you'll find the B vitamins and vitamins A, C, and E to support blood flow, metabolism, and hormone balance, along with the minerals iron, calcium, and potassium to promote the body's muscle maintenance and fat-burning process. Add to these benefits the ginger's stimulation of fat-burning potential with its slight spiciness that stokes the metabolic fire for increased fat loss and improved energy, and you've got the perfect ingredient combination for weight-loss nutrition.

Watermelon-Berry

The deliciousness of watermelon also comes with a wide variety of surprising nutrients including vitamin A, the B vitamins, vitamin C, and vitamin E, as well as calcium and iron, taking this infused water recipe to new heights with weight-loss-focused nutrition.

Ingredients | Yields 1 liter

1 liter water
½ cup peeled and chopped watermelon
¼ cup raspberries, muddled
¼ cup blueberries, muddled

1. Prepare a pitcher or water infuser product with 1 liter water.

2. Place the watermelon, raspberries, and blueberries inside the pitcher or water infuser's canister.

3. Allow mixture to steep in the refrigerator or a cool, dark place for 4–8 hours. For best flavor and health benefits, consume within 24–48 hours.

The Key Ingredients

Raspberries and blueberries further support weight-loss goals in a number of ways and with a variety of vitamins and minerals, but specifically with the benefits of their phytonutrients, anthocyanins and anthocyanadins. These powerful polyphenols act as potent antioxidants that promote blood health, support detoxification, and reduce respiratory infections and illnesses. The addition of these beautiful berries minimizes the stress on the respiratory system, allowing for better oxygen intake, improved carbon dioxide output (which is how fat is expelled from the body), and improved oxygen delivery throughout the body.

Chapter 7

Infusions for Boosting Energy

Who doesn't need a little help improving their energy levels once in a while? Without a doubt, there's no better way to improve your energy than naturally, using the nutrients available through vibrant whole foods. The fruits, spices, herbs, and teas that combine to create every delightful recipe in this chapter are brimming with energizing B vitamins, vitamin C, vitamin E, and countless minerals and phytochemicals that help support the processes responsible for energy production. These drinks will invigorate your body and mind, helping you to stay energized throughout your day without the jitters, highs, and crashes that so often accompany energy drinks, sugary beverages, and caffeine. By ensuring that your body has ample supplies of the nutrients it needs for cardiovascular health, nervous system health, mental functioning, proper digestion, and the body's processing and storing of these essential nutrients, you can safeguard your energy supply and better regulate your daily patterns so that you have enough energy during the day, sounder sleep at night, and an overall betterment of health that keeps you moving toward a more fit, more energized you!

Spiced Peaches and Plums

Sights and smells can invigorate the senses, awakening the body and mind.
With vibrant ingredients and sensational spice, this infused water recipe
makes for the perfect combination of sensations for the senses!

Ingredients | Yields 1 liter
1 liter water
1 cinnamon stick
1 teaspoon whole cloves
1 medium peach, peeled, pitted, and sliced
1 medium plum, peeled, pitted, and sliced

1. Prepare a pitcher or water infuser product with 1 liter water.

2. Place the cinnamon and cloves in a spice bag, and place the peach, plum, and spice bag inside the pitcher or water infuser's canister.

3. Allow mixture to steep in the refrigerator or a cool, dark place for 2–4 hours. For best flavor and health benefits, consume within 24–48 hours.

The Key Ingredients

Peaches and plums add sensational amounts of B vitamins and beta-carotene to every sip, combining vitamins and antioxidants that support the brain's health and the production of the feel-good hormones that keep your energy up throughout the day. Add to those benefits the spicy pleasures of cinnamon, which contributes a number of phytochemicals and phytonutrients to help regulate blood sugar and keep energy levels from spiking and dropping throughout the day.

Cherry–Passion Fruit

The nutrients of passion fruit combine with the cherries' rich anthocyanins, which act as potent antioxidants that protect the health of cells and promote their proper functioning, to form a splendidly sweet infused water recipe that not only gives you energy but also gives your taste buds a tropical treat.

Ingredients | Yields 1 liter

1 liter water
1 medium passion fruit, cut in half and flesh removed
½ cup pitted cherries

1. Prepare a pitcher or water infuser product with 1 liter water.

2. Place the flesh of the passion fruit and cherries inside the pitcher or water infuser's canister.

3. Allow mixture to steep in the refrigerator or a cool, dark place for 2–4 hours. For best flavor and health benefits, consume within 24–48 hours.

The Key Ingredients

Passion fruit are a tropical delight that can quickly and easily infuse your water with an array of powerful flavors, colors, and nutrients. The pulp found within the nutrient-dense passion fruit contains the vitamin A, B vitamins, vitamin C, iron, potassium, and a variety of antioxidants (including lycopene and cryptoxanthin) that can transform any simple bottle of water into liquid energy! Brimming with potent nutrients and powerful antioxidants, passion fruit is packed with a startling amount of iron, which helps to improve the hemoglobin in the blood and maximize oxygen delivery throughout the body and brain; this optimized oxygen delivery means less fatigue and more energy.

Pineapple-Apple-Grape

With crisp, refreshing fruits that help keep you energized, this infused water recipe is a taste sensation worth sipping!

Ingredients | Yields 1 liter

1 liter water
1 (½"-thick) slice of pineapple, peeled and chopped
½ medium Granny Smith apple, peeled, cored, and sliced
¼ cup Concord grapes, halved

1. Prepare a pitcher or water infuser product with 1 liter water.

2. Place the pineapple, apple, and grapes inside the pitcher or water infuser's canister.

3. Allow mixture to steep in the refrigerator or a cool, dark place for 2–4 hours. For best flavor and health benefits, consume within 24–48 hours.

The Key Ingredients

In order to have more energy, your cells, organs, and systems have to be functioning at their best. With this infused water recipe, you can ensure that your blood has the proper amount of iron, your brain has enough B vitamins, your immune system is being supported with adequate amounts of vitamin C, and your cells are being protected against oxidative stress that can lead to illness and fatigue. This delicious combination of pineapple, apple, and grapes helps your body and brain not only reap the immense benefits of all these essential nutrients, but also get a great dose of potassium, magnesium, and iron to help support the body's production of adenosine triphosphate (ATP), an essential in the production of energy.

Citrus-Apricot

In the quest for more energy, many people opt for sugar-laden beverages or energy drinks, but end up experiencing only a quick burst of energy that is inevitably followed by a "crash." Sweet and refreshing, this tropical combination will give you the energy you want without the crash you don't.

Ingredients | Yields 1 liter
1 liter water
1 medium tangerine, peeled and sliced
1 (½"-thick) slice of pineapple, peeled and chopped
1 medium apricot, peeled and pitted

1. Prepare a pitcher or water infuser product with 1 liter water.
2. Place the tangerine, pineapple, and apricot inside the pitcher or water infuser's canister.
3. Allow mixture to steep in the refrigerator or a cool, dark place for 2–4 hours. For best flavor and health benefits, consume within 24–48 hours.

The Key Ingredients

By combining sweet fruits such as tangerines, pineapple, and apricots that not only provide vitamin C, B vitamins, potassium, magnesium, and potent antioxidants, but also provide the body with glucose and fructose, energy levels go up and stay up. The glucose and fructose combination in these fruits, called disaccharides, work hand in hand to reduce insulin levels and maintain stable blood sugar levels for hours.

Cherry-Tangerine

These fruits support the brain's functioning and the production of feel-good chemicals that can keep you feeling energized and focused throughout your day!

Ingredients | Yields 1 liter
1 liter water
½ cup pitted cherries, chopped
2 medium tangerines, peeled and sliced

1. Prepare a pitcher or water infuser product with 1 liter water.

2. Place the cherries and tangerines inside the pitcher or water infuser's canister.

3. Allow mixture to steep in the refrigerator or a cool, dark place for 2–4 hours. For best flavor and health benefits, consume within 24–48 hours.

The Key Ingredients

Fatigue is one of the worst side effects of illness and infection. By safeguarding your cells' health against oxidative stress and protecting your immune system, you can help your body and brain function properly and enjoy lasting energy instead of focusing on fending off illness. Cherries and tangerines pair perfectly in this recipe to do just that, providing anthocyanadins and vitamin C that support the fight against illness and the boosting of healthy energy.

Pear-Grapefruit

When you're in need of a quick pick-me-up,
nothing seems to do the trick like sweet and tangy citrus.

Ingredients | Yields 1 liter

1 liter water
1 medium Bartlett pear, peeled, cored, and sliced
1 medium white grapefruit, peeled and sliced

1. Prepare a pitcher or water infuser product with 1 liter water.
2. Place the pear and grapefruit inside the pitcher or water infuser's canister.
3. Allow mixture to steep in the refrigerator or a cool, dark place for 2–4 hours. For best flavor and health benefits, consume within 24–48 hours.

The Key Ingredients

Rather than opting for sugar-laden store-bought juices made from concentrate and packed with additives, you can create a quick, delicious, all-natural infused water like this one. In every delicious dose, nutrients such as B vitamins, vitamin C, potassium, magnesium, and protective antioxidants from the grapefruit and pears help to stimulate the brain, detoxify the body, and maintain regular blood sugar levels throughout the day. This infusion will give you energy and avoid the slumps and bumps that can result when your body lacks the proper nutrition it needs and deserves.

Orange-Grapefruit-Melon

This infused water recipe contains delicious citrus and refreshing honeydew melon and has essential nutrients and powerful antioxidants that support cell health and immunity. Feeling energized and living healthfully never tasted so great!

Ingredients | Yields 1 liter
1 liter water
1 medium orange, peeled and sliced
½ large pink grapefruit, peeled and sliced
½ cup peeled and chopped honeydew melon

1. Prepare a pitcher or water infuser product with 1 liter water.

2. Place the orange, grapefruit, and honeydew inside the pitcher or water infuser's canister.

3. Allow mixture to steep in the refrigerator or a cool, dark place for 2–4 hours. For best flavor and health benefits, consume within 24–48 hours.

The Key Ingredients

You may wonder exactly what your body needs in order to supply the energy that lets you thrive all day and sleep well all night, enabling a routine that makes your life the happy and healthy one you've always desired. An array of vitamins—A, C, E, and the Bs—along with minerals potassium, magnesium, iron, and selenium all work together to ensure that the blood can transport abundant energy-producing oxygen and nutrients throughout the brain and body.

Watermelon-Kiwi-Pineapple

This recipe combines watermelon, kiwi, and pineapple for an energizing infused water that not only tastes great but also supports the systems involved with energy production, letting you keep your healthy body in motion.

Ingredients | Yields 1 liter

1 liter water
½ cup peeled and chopped watermelon
1 medium kiwi, peeled and sliced
1 (½"-thick) slice of pineapple, peeled and chopped

1. Prepare a pitcher or water infuser product with 1 liter water.

2. Place the watermelon, kiwi, and pineapple inside the pitcher or water infuser's canister.

3. Allow mixture to steep in the refrigerator or a cool, dark place for 2–4 hours. For best flavor and health benefits, consume within 24–48 hours.

The Key Ingredients

One of the nutrients the average person doesn't get enough of is protein. Protein works hand in hand with vitamins and minerals to ensure that the body has enough energy to engage in activity, thought, and the metabolic processes that allow the body to survive. This recipe also provides vitamins, minerals, and phytochemicals that act together to support metabolic functions, immunity, and cognitive processes, so you can enjoy a refreshing treat that helps you function at your best.

Pineapple-Apple-Plum

Packed with vibrant fruits, this recipe combines the flavors of pineapple, apple, and plum that each contributes its own nutrients to help your body produce and sustain energy morning to night!

Ingredients | Yields 1 liter

1 liter water
1 (½"-thick) slice of pineapple, peeled and chopped
½ medium Fuji apple, peeled, cored, and sliced
1 medium plum, peeled, pitted, and sliced

1. Prepare a pitcher or water infuser product with 1 liter water.

2. Place the pineapple, apple, and plum inside the pitcher or water infuser's canister.

3. Allow mixture to steep in the refrigerator or a cool, dark place for 2–4 hours. For best flavor and health benefits, consume within 24–48 hours.

The Key Ingredients

Pineapple's rich amounts of vitamin C pair with its unique phytochemical, bromelain, to help jump-start mental functioning while also providing powerful antioxidant protection. Apples offer their own special phytochemical, quercetin, which helps support respiratory functioning, ensuring that the blood and brain have adequate supplies of oxygen (a must for energy production!). Plums add vitamin A and the powerful phytochemical beta-carotene that is used throughout the body to support the immune system and protect the cells from stress, illness, and disease, all of which can zap energy in a flash!

Grape-Grapefruit-Lime

Even as you prepare the ingredients to create this infused water recipe, the stimulating aromas of these fruits allow you to see, smell, and feel the invigorating nutrients that give your body and brain the energy they need to thrive.

Ingredients | Yields 1 liter

1 liter water
½ cup halved red grapes
½ medium pink grapefruit, peeled and sliced
1 large lime, peeled and sliced

1. Prepare a pitcher or water infuser product with 1 liter water.

2. Place the grapes, grapefruit, and lime inside the pitcher or water infuser's canister.

3. Allow mixture to steep in the refrigerator or a cool, dark place for 2–4 hours. For best flavor and health benefits, consume within 24–48 hours.

The Key Ingredients

This water offers the illness prevention and health promotion your body needs in order to thrive. Sweet grapes provide antioxidants that safeguard cell health, cleanse the blood of impurities, and promote cell regeneration. The grapefruit and lime are energy-stimulating, vitamin C–packed, antioxidant-rich citrus fruits that help awaken the senses, protect the processes involved in energy production, and help maintain a stable blood sugar level that allows you to move smoothly through your day.

Green Tea with Cherries and Lime

Green tea is one of the most antioxidant-rich sources in the world, providing the body with an array of powerful protectors against free radical damage and oxidative stress that can wreak havoc on the body's cells and immune system.

Ingredients | Yields 1 liter

1 liter water
2 organic green tea bags
½ cup pitted cherries, chopped
1 large lime, peeled and sliced

1. Prepare a pitcher or water infuser product with 1 liter water.

2. Place the tea bags, cherries, and lime inside the pitcher or water infuser's canister.

3. Allow mixture to steep in the refrigerator or a cool, dark place for 2–4 hours. For best flavor and health benefits, consume within 24–48 hours.

The Key Ingredients

Another benefit of green tea is one that can greatly improve your energy levels naturally: caffeine. When you include green tea in an infused water recipe like this one, you not only improve the health benefits but also reap the reward of naturally stimulating green tea. With the addition of sweet, tart anthocyanadin-rich cherries and limonin-packed lime, you have a recipe that perks you up while keeping your body and brain free of toxins, and reduces debilitating cellular damage.

Green Tea with Grapefruit and Mint

Packed with antioxidants and a wide variety of polyphenols that support every-thing from immunity and brain functioning to cell and cardiovascular health, green tea is one of the must-have infusion ingredients for healthy living.

Ingredients | Yields 1 liter
1 liter water
2 organic green tea bags
1 medium white grapefruit, peeled and sliced
¼ cup mint leaves, chopped

1. Prepare a pitcher or water infuser product with 1 liter water.

2. Place the tea bags, grapefruit, and mint inside the pitcher or water infuser's canister.

3. Allow mixture to steep in the refrigerator or a cool, dark place for 2–4 hours. For best flavor and health benefits, consume within 24–48 hours.

The Key Ingredients

Green tea's contribution of natural caffeine stimulates the mind and body naturally, helping to energize and stabilize those energy levels while you sip your infused water throughout the day. The B vitamins and vitamin C in the grapefruit and the rosmarinic acid in the mint combine to make this recipe one that takes energy and overall health to new heights, while softening the slightly bitter taste of plain green tea.

Chapter 8

Infusions for Gut Health and Reduced Inflammation

Few people are aware of the importance of gut health and a diet and lifestyle combination geared toward reducing inflammation. Within the gut, not only is digestion taking place, but so are countless functions that allow the body to process, distribute, store, and produce nutrients that are needed for every function of the body. With natural whole fruits, vegetables, herbs, teas, and spices, the gut is able to process foods with ease, digest them easily, extract astounding amounts of naturally occurring nutrients, and then use those nutrients for the body's needs. While these vibrant, natural foods help support the body's functions like detoxification, cardiovascular functioning, nerve impulses and communication, and immunity, they are also helping to reduce the levels of inflammation throughout the body and its systems. Chronic inflammation that can be felt in joints, tendons, muscles, and skin, and the inflammation that is systemic and goes unseen, can cause the body to develop chronic diseases including arthritis and even certain types of cancer. By combining the antioxidant-rich, anti-inflammatory-packed foods in the infused water recipes of this chapter, you can help return your gut health to optimal levels and reduce your inflammation, pain, and systemic issues that can be caused or exaggerated by inflammation.

Gingered Blue Raspberry

Focusing on a diet that is void of unhealthy sweeteners, unhealthy fats, and unhealthy additives can reduce inflammation naturally, helping you restore total health to your body and mind.

Ingredients | Yields 1 liter

1 liter water
1" piece ginger, peeled and sliced
½ cup blueberries, lightly muddled
½ cup raspberries, lightly muddled

1. Prepare a pitcher or water infuser product with 1 liter water.

2. Place the ginger, blueberries, and raspberries inside the pitcher or water infuser's canister.

3. Allow mixture to steep in the refrigerator or a cool, dark place for 2–4 hours. For best flavor and health benefits, consume within 24–48 hours.

The Key Ingredients

Anti-inflammatory properties abound in every last sip of this delicious infused water recipe thanks to ginger's naturally occurring compounds gingerol and shogaol, and the anthocyanins and anthocyanadins of blueberries and raspberries. These ingredients create a trifecta of inflammation-fighting compounds that not only fight inflammation at the site but also improve immunity and support overall health. Natural inflammation fighting . . . with an amazing taste!

Strawberry-Cucumber with Mint

With anti-inflammatory properties in every one of the delightful ingredients in this recipe, inflammation doesn't stand a chance! This water infused with sweet treats and refreshing mint will not only help you feel better, it will do it deliciously.

Ingredients | Yields 1 liter

1 liter water
6 strawberries, tops removed and sliced
3" piece cucumber, peeled and sliced
¼ cup mint leaves, chopped

1. Prepare a pitcher or water infuser product with 1 liter water.

2. Place the strawberries, cucumber, and mint inside the pitcher or water infuser's canister.

3. Allow mixture to steep in the refrigerator or a cool, dark place for 2–4 hours. For best flavor and health benefits, consume within 24–48 hours.

The Key Ingredients

Strawberries contribute vitamins and minerals that support overall health and promote healthy digestion, a must in the fight against inflammation. They also contain vitamin C and anthocyanins that not only give strawberries their vibrant hue, but act as powerful antioxidants and anti-inflammatory compounds. Cucumber adds an array of vitamins and minerals, but also combats oxidative stress within cells that can contribute to the aggravation of inflammation. Mint has a unique phytochemical, rosmarinic acid, that acts as a powerful anti-inflammatory agent, blocking the pro-inflammation chemicals that can wreak havoc throughout the body.

Spiced-So-Nice Cherry

Cherries are a wonder food in the world of inflammation! Additionally this recipe contains an array of nutrients that promote health within the brain, body, and especially the gut.

Ingredients | Yields 1 liter
1 liter water
1 cup pitted and chopped cherries
1 cinnamon stick
1 teaspoon whole cloves

1. Prepare a pitcher or water infuser product with 1 liter water.

2. Place the cloves inside a spice bag, and place the cherries, cinnamon, and spice bag inside the pitcher or water infuser's canister.

3. Allow mixture to steep in the refrigerator or a cool, dark place for 2–4 hours. For best flavor and health benefits, consume within 24–48 hours.

The Key Ingredients

The rich anthocyanins that give cherries their deep red coloring have antioxidant and anti-inflammatory benefits that move throughout the body—scavenging toxins, fending off free radicals, supporting cell health and repair, and fighting pro-inflammatory chemicals and existing inflammation. Adding to the potency of cherries are the cinnamon and cloves. Not only delicious, these spices both deliver antimicrobial benefits that support the immune system, and cloves also provide omega-3 fatty acids, which are highly recommended in the fight against inflammation.

Gingered Green Tea with Watermelon

Including ginger in your infusion recipes is a great way to spice up your water while reaping some major benefits in all areas of your health. This recipe creates a sweet treat of infused water bliss that can please your taste buds and improve your health!

Ingredients | Yields 1 liter

1 liter water
2 organic green tea bags
1" piece ginger, peeled and sliced
1 cup peeled and chopped watermelon

1. Prepare a pitcher or water infuser product with 1 liter water.

2. Place the tea bags, ginger, and watermelon inside the pitcher or water infuser's canister.

3. Allow mixture to steep in the refrigerator or a cool, dark place for 2–4 hours. For best flavor and health benefits, consume within 24–48 hours.

The Key Ingredients

Ginger's unique compounds shogaol and gingerol act as powerful antioxidants, anti-inflammatory agents, and antimicrobial compounds to improve your body's functioning and promote and protect the body's healing and recovery from inflammation. Green tea contributes a powerful antioxidant called epigallocatechin gallate (EGCG) that fights free radical damage, improves immunity, and also reduces inflammation. Watermelon adds a healthy dose of vitamin C, the B vitamins, and vitamin A, as well as potassium and magnesium.

Fruity Fig and Apple

Figs and apples make this infusion a sweet and refreshing treat, filled with powerful nutrition that will not only maximize your health through improved immunity and better blood flow, but will also help you alleviate inflammation and provide your gut with the nutrition it needs.

Ingredients | Yields 1 liter

1 liter water
6 strawberries, tops removed and sliced
1 medium fig, peeled and chopped
½ medium Granny Smith apple, peeled, cored, and sliced

1. Prepare a pitcher or water infuser product with 1 liter water.

2. Place the strawberries, fig, and apple inside the pitcher or water infuser's canister.

3. Allow mixture to steep in the refrigerator or a cool, dark place for 2–4 hours. For best flavor and health benefits, consume within 24–48 hours.

The Key Ingredients

Naturally occurring B vitamins and vitamins C, D, and E as well as minerals calcium, magnesium, and potassium join with unique antioxidants and phytochemicals such as the apple's quercetin in this recipe. Together, they help stimulate proper digestion, improve delivery of nutrients throughout the body, heal inflammation, and prevent oxidative stress in the gut and the rest of the body.

Gingered Beet Treat

The spiciness of ginger takes the sweet flavors of beets to new heights in this delicious and healthful infused water recipe.

Ingredients | Yields 1 liter

1 liter water
1" piece ginger, peeled and sliced
1 medium red beet, top removed and sliced
1 medium golden beet, top removed and sliced

1. Prepare a pitcher or water infuser product with 1 liter water.

2. Place the ginger and beets inside the pitcher or water infuser's canister.

3. Allow mixture to steep in the refrigerator or a cool, dark place for 2–4 hours. For best flavor and health benefits, consume within 24–48 hours.

The Key Ingredients

This blend helps the body to detoxify impurities and produce and process hormones, as well as assisting the digestive system in its various functions. Ginger's oils and enzymes couple with beets' potent antioxidants and anti-inflammatory compounds to help cleanse the body of the pro-inflammatory chemicals and compounds that contribute to the development or worsening of inflammation. With sweet flavors from red and golden beets and a kick of spice delivered by ginger, this infused water recipe is a great addition to any diet focused on reducing inflammation and promoting gut health.

Figgy Cucumber-Citrus

Sweet figs combine with subtle cucumber and splendid citrus for a great-tasting infused water that contributes to the reduction of inflammation and to the optimized health of the gut.

Ingredients | Yields 1 liter

1 liter water
1 medium fig, peeled and sliced
3" piece cucumber, peeled and sliced
1 medium tangerine, peeled and sliced

1. Prepare a pitcher or water infuser product with 1 liter water.

2. Place the fig, cucumber, and tangerine inside the pitcher or water infuser's canister.

3. Allow mixture to steep in the refrigerator or a cool, dark place for 2–4 hours. For best flavor and health benefits, consume within 24–48 hours.

The Key Ingredients

Inside this infusion are powerful nutrients and polyphenols that scavenge free radicals and pro-inflammatory compounds from the blood. These ingredients also minimize the risk of infections by contributing antioxidants and vitamin C, and by helping to keep the gut clear of bad bacteria, microbes, and viruses that can lead to a variety of illnesses and uncomfortable conditions. This recipe also keeps the body and gut free of inflammation that can lead to inflammatory conditions of the gut and bowels and pain and discomfort of the joints.

Raspberry-Blackberry-Acai

Rich in powerful antioxidants, these three berries contribute to the health and well-being of the entire body with every sweet drop of this infused water.

Ingredients | Yields 1 liter

1 liter water
½ cup raspberries, lightly muddled
½ cup blackberries, lightly muddled
¼ cup acai berries

1. Prepare a pitcher or water infuser product with 1 liter water.

2. Place the raspberries, blackberries, and acai berries inside the pitcher or water infuser's canister.

3. Allow mixture to steep in the refrigerator or a cool, dark place for 2–4 hours. For best flavor and health benefits, consume within 24–48 hours.

The Key Ingredients

Helping to combat the illnesses that can result from oxidative stress and free radical damage to the cells, the naturally occurring phytochemicals and polyphenols—anthocyanins, anthocyanadins, and ferulic acid—make this fruity concoction a delicious way to minimize inflammation everywhere from the lungs to the joints. This blend benefits your body and brain with antioxidant, anti-inflammatory, and antimicrobial protection that ensures you stay free of illness and disease and can maintain a healthy life free of pain and discomfort.

Sweet Beet and Cherry

Sweet cherries and vibrant beets combine to create a sensational infused water recipe that's a tempting treat for the taste buds and the eyes.

Ingredients | Yields 1 liter

1 liter water
1 medium golden beet, top removed and sliced
½ cup pitted and chopped cherries

1. Prepare a pitcher or water infuser product with 1 liter water.

2. Place the beet and cherries inside the pitcher or water infuser's canister.

3. Allow mixture to steep in the refrigerator or a cool, dark place for 2–4 hours. For best flavor and health benefits, consume within 24–48 hours.

The Key Ingredients

Beets are nature's cleanser. This underappreciated vegetable is high in magnesium, potassium, fiber, iron, vitamins A, B, and C, not to mention beta-carotene, betacyanin, and folic acid. Beets are also a good source of the phytonutrients betanin and vulgaxanthin, which provide anti-inflammatory, antioxidant, and detoxification support. Beets help purify the blood, work wonders on cleansing the liver, help you maintain good heart health, and can help prevent several forms of cancer including colon cancer. Combine all these benefits with the potent phytochemicals in cherries that combat pro-inflammatory compounds and you've got a drink that will treat whatever ails you!

Cherry-Berry-Citrus

Regarded as one of the most effective foods in fighting inflammation, sweet and slightly tart cherries take center stage in this delicious infused water recipe.

Ingredients | Yields 1 liter

1 liter water
½ cup pitted and chopped cherries
¼ cup blueberries, lightly muddled
1 large lemon, peeled and sliced

1. Prepare a pitcher or water infuser product with 1 liter water.

2. Place the cherries, blueberries, and lemon inside the pitcher or water infuser's canister.

3. Allow mixture to steep in the refrigerator or a cool, dark place for 2–4 hours. For best flavor and health benefits, consume within 24–48 hours.

The Key Ingredients

Cherries—with their potent phytochemicals that combat pro-inflammatory compounds—team up with antioxidant-rich blueberries and vitamin C–packed lemon for a sweet treat that helps promote the health and proper functioning of the cells, organs, and systems, while boosting the immune system, combating illness and disease, and preventing inflammation from occurring throughout the body. Proper water intake further supports the nutrients of this recipe's ingredients by hydrating your cells and promoting the immune system's defenses against illness and disease, thus helping you to achieve a better-functioning body with optimal levels of health throughout.

Lemony Mango-Berry with Apple Cider Vinegar

Gingivitis and infections within the mouth and gums can lead to inflammation throughout the body, especially the gut. Luckily, the ingredients in this infused water can help you improve your oral health while introducing specific nutrients that minimize inflammation naturally in your entire body.

Ingredients | Yields 1 liter
1 liter water
½ large lemon, peeled and sliced
½ cup peeled and sliced mango
¼ cup blueberries, lightly muddled
1 tablespoon organic, unfiltered, unpasteurized apple cider vinegar

1. Prepare a pitcher or water infuser product with 1 liter water.

2. Place the lemon, mango, blueberries, and vinegar inside the pitcher or water infuser's canister.

3. Allow mixture to steep in the refrigerator or a cool, dark place for 2–4 hours. For best flavor and health benefits, consume within 24–48 hours.

The Key Ingredients

Contributing to stomach issues, digestive complications, and irritation and inflammation within the gut, oral health is an area that should be properly cared for to reduce inflammation. The lemons contain naturally occurring vitamin C that acts to fight infection. The antioxidants and anti-inflammatory compounds from the mango and berries and the enzymes within the apple cider vinegar act to fight free radical damage, fend off bacteria and microbes that commonly cause infections in the mouth, and even promote the gut's health with probiotic benefits.

Ginger-Peach with Apple Cider Vinegar

The sweet flavors of peaches get intensified with the addition of spicy ginger and slightly tart apple cider vinegar for a taste sensation that provides health benefits galore. This delightful combination delivers powerful nutrition that tastes great and makes you feel great, too!

Ingredients | Yields 1 liter

1 liter water
1" piece ginger, peeled and sliced
2 medium peaches, peeled, pitted, and sliced
1 tablespoon organic, unfiltered, unpasteurized apple cider vinegar

1. Prepare a pitcher or water infuser product with 1 liter water.

2. Place the ginger, peaches, and vinegar inside the pitcher or water infuser's canister.

3. Allow mixture to steep in the refrigerator or a cool, dark place for 2–4 hours. For best flavor and health benefits, consume within 24–48 hours.

The Key Ingredients

Peaches delight the senses with their vibrant yellow hue that signifies the strong presence of beta-carotene. Added to that potent antioxidant are the naturally occurring compounds of ginger—gingerol and shogaol—and enzymes of the apple cider vinegar, all of which contribute to the fight against free radical damage and pro-inflammatory compounds. This recipe's powerful ingredients help promote healthy functioning of the body's cells, organs, and systems while providing protection against the proteins and compounds that can wreak havoc on health.

Chapter 9

Infusions for Stress Relief and Improved Mental Functioning

Without the stress-induced distraction, depression, and anxiety that often lead to scattered thoughts and inability to focus, you can live a healthier, happier, and more gratifying existence. You can use clean, whole foods, herbs, and spices to naturally reduce stress levels and improve mental functioning. Bright colorful produce and herbs contain naturally occurring polyphenols that give their flesh and exterior vibrant hues. The body uses these polyphenols to produce vitamins, utilize minerals, protect the cells against harmful oxidative stress, fend off illness, and even reduce inflammation. When the body is under stress, countless physical processes are adversely affected, which then contributes to physical and mental issues that further contribute to stress, creating a vicious cycle. Luckily, you can use nutrition to stop the cycle permanently. By using the infused water recipes in this chapter, you can deliver nutrients such as vitamin A, B vitamins, vitamin C, and vitamin E, along with minerals such as iron, calcium, selenium, and magnesium, and phytochemicals such as antioxidants and anti-inflammatory agents. These vitamins and minerals work to improve the brain's and body's production of feel-good chemicals, safeguard the body from the depletion and misuse of nutrients, and support the body's systems that are directly involved with stress and mental functioning.

Cranberry Chamomile with Orange

With the delicious flavors of tart cranberries and sweet citrus, this recipe's star ingredient, chamomile tea, makes a splendid drink that maximizes mental functioning naturally.

Ingredients | Yields 1 liter

1 liter water
2 chamomile tea bags
½ cup cranberries, crushed (and resulting juice)
1 medium orange, peeled and sliced

1. Prepare a pitcher or water infuser product with 1 liter water.

2. Place the tea bags, cranberries (and their juice), and orange inside the pitcher or water infuser's canister.

3. Allow mixture to steep in the refrigerator or a cool, dark place for 2–4 hours. For best flavor and health benefits, consume within 24–48 hours.

The Key Ingredients

Chamomile tea provides benefits galore with its flavonoids, such as chrysin, which not only combat inflammation and fight infection but also promote the production of feel-good hormones such as dopamine and serotonin in the brain. The cranberries and orange add vitamin C, B vitamins, iron, and potassium, which contribute to the proper functioning of the nervous system, help to reduce anxiety, and restore a sense of calm.

Blackberry Black Tea with Ginger

Blackberry tea is rich in a number of powerful antioxidants that protect the cells from free radical damage, and also has an amino acid, L-theanine, that helps to reduce anxiety and increase alpha brain waves that relax the brain and reduce stress.

Ingredients | Yields 1 liter
1 liter water
2 black tea bags
1 cup blackberries, lightly muddled
1" piece ginger, peeled and sliced

1. Prepare a pitcher or water infuser product with 1 liter water.
2. Place the tea bags, blackberries, and ginger inside the pitcher or water infuser's canister.
3. Allow mixture to steep in the refrigerator or a cool, dark place for 2–4 hours. For best flavor and health benefits, consume within 24–48 hours.

The Key Ingredients

Few people realize how severely the mental processes can be impacted by toxins and free radical–induced cellular oxidative stress. This infusion, spiced perfectly with delicious ginger and sweet blackberries, provides the body and brain with B vitamins, iron, potassium, and magnesium, helping to promote feel-good hormone production while ridding the body and brain of toxins that can degrade cell health and mental processes.

Kiwi-Cantaloupe with Blueberries and Sage

Not only is this infused water recipe filled with potent protective antioxidants that prevent oxidative stress on the cells, but the ingredients also contribute a plethora of nutrients that directly affect the brain's functioning.

Ingredients | Yields 1 liter
1 liter water
1 medium kiwi, peeled and sliced
¼ cup peeled and chopped cantaloupe
½ cup blueberries, lightly muddled
3 sage leaves, chopped

1. Prepare a pitcher or water infuser product with 1 liter water.
2. Place the kiwi, cantaloupe, blueberries, and sage inside the pitcher or water infuser's canister.
3. Allow mixture to steep in the refrigerator or a cool, dark place for 2–4 hours. For best flavor and health benefits, consume within 24–48 hours.

The Key Ingredients

This infusion contains B vitamins, vitamin C, and vitamin E, as well as minerals zinc and selenium, all of which help provide the brain with nutrients for proper functioning and proper hormone production. Vitamin C–rich kiwi and beta-carotene-packed cantaloupe combine with the potent anthocyanins of blueberries and phytochemicals of sage in a powerful combination of nutrients that safeguards the cells and immune system and supports the brain chemicals that reduce stress and relieve anxiety.

Raspberry-Honeydew with Basil

The unique taste of basil pairs with raspberries and honeydew to create a trifecta of nutrient-dense ingredients that help maintain the brain's health and well-being, letting you reap the benefits of a less stressed and more focused experience.

Ingredients | Yields 1 liter
1 liter water
½ cup raspberries, lightly muddled
½ cup peeled and chopped honeydew melon
¼ cup basil leaves, chopped

1. Prepare a pitcher or water infuser product with 1 liter water.

2. Place the raspberries, honeydew, and basil inside the pitcher or water infuser's canister.

3. Allow mixture to steep in the refrigerator or a cool, dark place for 2–4 hours. For best flavor and health benefits, consume within 24–48 hours.

The Key Ingredients

As a staple of ancient Ayurvedic medicine for its chemical compounds that contribute to the reduction of everything from inflammation to anxiety, basil has a reputation for restoring health to many areas of the body, and rightfully so. Scientific studies have shown basil to contain naturally occurring oils, enzymes, and polyphenols that act as potent antioxidants. These antioxidants scavenge the brain, body, and blood of free radicals, protecting the cells, organs, and systems against dangerous oxidative stress that can deplete feel-good hormones, endanger hormone production, and compromise the nervous system.

Lemon-Lime-Cilantro

Citrusy and spicy, this infused water recipe is a winner, not merely for its taste but also for its impressive benefits to the brain and body that can help you live a happier, healthier life naturally.

Ingredients | Yields 1 liter
1 liter water
1 large lemon, peeled and sliced
1 large lime, peeled and sliced
¼ cup cilantro, chopped

1. Prepare a pitcher or water infuser product with 1 liter water.

2. Place the lemon, lime, and cilantro inside the pitcher or water infuser's canister.

3. Allow mixture to steep in the refrigerator or a cool, dark place for 2–4 hours. For best flavor and health benefits, consume within 24–48 hours.

The Key Ingredients

Lemon and lime contribute the potent free radical–fighting antioxidant benefits of their vitamin C to this recipe. The powerful antioxidant protection provided by vitamin C is boosted by the rich stores of nutrients and naturally occurring polyphenols and flavonoids in cilantro. Cilantro contributes a plentiful array of oils including cymene, terpineol, and linalool; antioxidants quercetin, rhamnetin, and apigenin; and calcium, potassium, and magnesium to further support the processes of the brain, nervous system, and hormone production, contributing to the reduction of stress and anxiety.

Very Berry Chamomile with Lime

The refreshing taste of chamomile blends with the bright flavors of berries and lime in this infused water recipe that provides the body and brain with protection and performance-enhancing nutrition. This recipe is the perfect prescription for anyone in need of natural balance.

Ingredients | Yields 1 liter

1 liter water
2 chamomile tea bags
¼ cup blueberries, lightly muddled
¼ cup raspberries, lightly muddled
¼ cup blackberries, lightly muddled
½ large lime, peeled and sliced

1. Prepare a pitcher or water infuser product with 1 liter water.
2. Place the tea bags, blueberries, raspberries, blackberries, and lime inside the pitcher or water infuser's canister.
3. Allow mixture to steep in the refrigerator or a cool, dark place for 2–4 hours. For best flavor and health benefits, consume within 24–48 hours.

The Key Ingredients

This infusion helps to provide the body and brain with nutrients including B vitamins, vitamins C and E, and minerals such as iron, calcium, magnesium, and potassium to benefit overall health through improved immune system functioning. It also protects and preserves the health of the cells, organs, and systems involved with the processes that contribute to cognitive functioning and balanced hormone production. The result: less stress and anxiety, better sleep habits, and an overall improvement in energy levels and the ability to focus throughout the day.

Cool Cucumber-Basil-Melon

Lending little flavor but lots of nutrition, cucumber pairs up with antioxidant-rich melon and basil for a truly tremendous brain-boosting recipe that provides not only vitamins and minerals but antioxidants too.

Ingredients | Yields 1 liter
1 liter water
3" piece cucumber, peeled and sliced
½ cup peeled and chopped honeydew melon
¼ cup basil leaves, chopped

1. Prepare a pitcher or water infuser product with 1 liter water.
2. Place the cucumber, honeydew, and basil inside the pitcher or water infuser's canister.
3. Allow mixture to steep in the refrigerator or a cool, dark place for 2–4 hours. For best flavor and health benefits, consume within 24–48 hours.

The Key Ingredients

The honeydew provides rich provisions of vitamin C, B vitamins, and an assortment of minerals including iron and calcium that contribute to the proper functioning of the brain's natural processes and communication with the nervous system. Basil adds a healthy dose of antioxidants to protect the cells from oxidative stress, which can degrade their health and ability to function properly. Sipping your way to better health and maximized brain benefits has never been so simple and delicious!

Gingered Cherry with Vanilla

The spiciness of ginger and aromatics of vanilla take the sensational flavors of cherries to new heights. Brimming with natural nutrition that supports mental health, the potent antioxidants in this infused water recipe help everything from hormone production to cell health.

Ingredients | Yields 1 liter
1 liter water
1 vanilla bean
1" piece ginger, peeled and sliced
1 cup pitted and chopped cherries

1. Prepare a pitcher or water infuser product with 1 liter water.

2. Slice the vanilla bean along the seam to expose the seeds, and place into a spice bag.

3. Place the spice bag, cherries, and ginger inside the pitcher or water infuser's canister.

4. Allow mixture to steep in the refrigerator or a cool, dark place for 2–4 hours. For best flavor and health benefits, consume within 24–48 hours.

The Key Ingredients

Ginger's natural oils and its compounds gingerol and shogaol help to safeguard the health of cells, organs, and systems from the disease and degradation that can be caused by oxidative stress. Cherries' antioxidants offer protection against infections, and their rich supply of magnesium, potassium, and calcium promotes the proper functioning of the nervous system. Rounding out the recipe's benefits is vanilla's potent phytochemical, vanillin. This recipe helps you achieve optimal health by ensuring that your energy levels, cognitive functioning, and feel-good hormone production reach and remain at optimal levels.

Pineapple-Pomegranate with Sage

Abundant in phytochemicals that combat free radical damage, this combination of sweet treats makes for a hydrating experience that prevents illness while promoting brain function naturally.

Ingredients | Yields 1 liter

1 liter water
1 (½"-thick) slice of pineapple, peeled and chopped
½ cup pomegranate jewels, muddled
2 sage leaves

1. Prepare a pitcher or water infuser product with 1 liter water.

2. Place the pineapple, pomegranate, and sage leaves inside the pitcher or water infuser's canister.

3. Allow mixture to steep in the refrigerator or a cool, dark place for 2–4 hours. For best flavor and health benefits, consume within 24–48 hours.

The Key Ingredients

Brimming with B vitamins and vitamins A, C, and E, this recipe provides the brain with minerals, protective antioxidants, and anti-inflammatory compounds that combine to support the immune system and promote healthy hormone production. This recipe also protects the cells against free radical damage that can compromise their functioning and ability to communicate with the nervous system and brain. Refreshing and invigorating, this combination is a great way to keep energy levels up and cognitive functioning at its best, and to maintain a healthy lifestyle free of stress, anxiety, and toxicity.

Strawberry Chamomile with Lemon

The delightful flavors of chamomile tea get sweetened and spiced with the delicious flavors of strawberries and citrus in this infused water recipe that contributes nutrients to target the health of the body and mind.

Ingredients | Yields 1 liter

1 liter water
2 chamomile tea bags
10 strawberries, tops removed and sliced
1 large lemon, peeled and sliced

1. Prepare a pitcher or water infuser product with 1 liter water.

2. Place the tea bags, strawberries, and lemon inside the pitcher or water infuser's canister.

3. Allow mixture to steep in the refrigerator or a cool, dark place for 2–4 hours. For best flavor and health benefits, consume within 24–48 hours.

The Key Ingredients

Potent antioxidants from each ingredient help to prevent free radical damage and oxidative stress that can wreak havoc on the processes having to do with hormone production, improved immunity, and brain function. The B vitamins, vitamins A, C, and E, along with minerals iron, magnesium, calcium, and potassium, join forces in this recipe with potent antioxidants for a flavorful infusion that boosts brain functioning, maintains cell integrity, and provides the body with the essential amino acids needed to create the feel-good hormones, boosting energy levels and reducing stress and anxiety naturally.

Sparkling Fig

The nutrients in figs and ginger help to minimize stress and anxiety while maintaining healthy communication between the brain and nervous system for better brain functioning and improved cognitive processes.

Ingredients | Yields 1 liter
1 liter water
3 medium figs, peeled and sliced
2" piece ginger, peeled and sliced

1. Prepare a pitcher or water infuser product with 1 liter water.

2. Place the figs and ginger inside the pitcher or water infuser's canister.

3. Allow mixture to steep in the refrigerator or a cool, dark place for 2–4 hours. For best flavor and health benefits, consume within 24–48 hours.

The Key Ingredients

Ginger's natural provisions of the unique compounds gingerol and shogaol join with B vitamins, potassium, and magnesium from the figs to create a perfectly paired prescription for brain health and optimized mental functioning. Protecting the brain's simplest components against harmful free radical degradation and oxidative stress, the antioxidants prevent harm while the vitamins and minerals combine to promote proper functioning and support hormone production of both serotonin and dopamine.

Raspberry Chamomile with Lemon and Lime

Sweet raspberries and luscious lemons and limes pair with calming chamomile for an amazing health-improving infusion that improves the immune system and your mental functioning as well.

Ingredients | Yields 1 liter
1 liter water
2 chamomile tea bags
½ cup raspberries, lightly muddled
1 large lemon, peeled and sliced
1 large lime, peeled and sliced

1. Prepare a pitcher or water infuser product with 1 liter water.
2. Place the tea bags, raspberries, lemon, and lime inside the pitcher or water infuser's canister.
3. Allow mixture to steep in the refrigerator or a cool, dark place for 2–4 hours. For best flavor and health benefits, consume within 24–48 hours.

The Key Ingredients

This infused water helps improve the immune system's ability to combat infection, illness, and disease, and also promotes the processes associated with energy levels, focus, and proper cognitive functioning. With rich provisions of viable vitamins, minerals, protective antioxidants, preventative anti-inflammatory compounds, and stores of powerful polyphenols that strengthen and support the production and processing of the feel-good hormones serotonin and dopamine, this blend of ingredients makes for a mindfully focused sweet treat filled with health benefits.

Chapter 10

Infusions for Men's and Women's Health

Men and women experience a variety of different health conditions, complications, and threats that affect one gender more than the other. For example, women have a higher incidence of breast cancer and osteoporosis while men have a higher rate of prostate cancer and colon cancer. While the conditions that strike one gender more than the other may be different, the nutrients that can be used by the body to fight off these conditions are, remarkably, the same. With the infused water recipes in this chapter, you'll find that a surprising number of fruits, vegetables, herbs, spices, teas, and additions can provide men and women with powerful nutrients such as B vitamins, vitamins A, C, and E, iron, calcium, magnesium, and an array of potent antioxidants and anti-inflammatory compounds. All of these nutrients can help safeguard health by boosting immunity and fighting the causes and conditions associated with the shared health issues, as well as those that are unique to each gender. With every delicious sip of these infused water recipes, men and women alike can enjoy a number of nutritional benefits that can improve their health and quality of life.

Black Tea with Cherries and Ginger

This recipe contains a number of phytochemicals and nutrients that combine to create a health-boosting line of defense that deters unhealthy cellular changes, illnesses, chronic diseases, and uncomfortable conditions that can strike both men and women.

Ingredients | Yields 1 liter
1 liter water
2 black tea bags
1 cup pitted and chopped cherries
1" piece ginger, peeled and sliced

1. Prepare a pitcher or water infuser product with 1 liter water.
2. Place the tea bags, cherries, and ginger inside the pitcher or water infuser's canister.
3. Allow mixture to steep in the refrigerator or a cool, dark place for 2–4 hours. For best flavor and health benefits, consume within 24–48 hours.

The Key Ingredients

Black tea contains L-theanine, a potent amino acid that helps to relax the brain, reduce stress, and calm anxiety. Adding antioxidant-rich cherries and enzyme-packed ginger makes a trio of ingredients that helps prevent inflammation, oxidative distress to cells, and possible development of cancerous changes in cells and organs. Even more benefits come from the blend's B vitamins, vitamins C and E, and calcium, potassium, and magnesium, further supporting the body's muscles, bones, and tissues and ensuring that these structures stay healthy.

Cherry-Fennel with Cilantro

Enhancing this recipe's flavor are the health benefits that come from each ingredient's powerful nutrients, which supply the bodies of men and women alike with the nutrients they need to combat illness and promote health and well-being.

Ingredients | Yields 1 liter

1 liter water
¾ cup pitted and chopped cherries
¼ cup sliced fennel
¼ cup cilantro, chopped

1. Prepare a pitcher or water infuser product with 1 liter water.

2. Place the cherries, fennel, and cilantro inside the pitcher or water infuser's canister.

3. Allow mixture to steep in the refrigerator or a cool, dark place for 2–4 hours. For best flavor and health benefits, consume within 24–48 hours.

The Key Ingredients

The supportive nutrition of B vitamins, vitamin C, and vitamin E can protect the cells of the brain and body from degradation and harmful oxidative stress. Calcium, magnesium, and potassium can aid in preserving mental well-being, bone density, muscle mass, and digestive function, which can all suffer as we age. Add to all this the boost of powerful antioxidants in this infusion and you are on your way to living a healthier, better quality of life.

Jalapeño-Cucumber with Pineapple

Enjoy vibrant flavor and healthy doses of vitamin A and vitamin C in this blend, as well as the unique antioxidants of the star ingredients, jalapeño and pineapple.

Ingredients | Yields 1 liter

1 liter water
½ medium jalapeño pepper, deseeded and sliced
3" piece cucumber, peeled and sliced
1 (½"-thick) slice of pineapple, peeled and chopped

1. Prepare a pitcher or water infuser product with 1 liter water.

2. Place the jalapeño, cucumber, and pineapple inside the pitcher or water infuser's canister.

3. Allow mixture to steep in the refrigerator or a cool, dark place for 2–4 hours. For best flavor and health benefits, consume within 24–48 hours.

The Key Ingredients

Jalapeños contain capsaicin, a powerful phytochemical that not only protects cell health but fights inflammation, improves blood health, and improves blood flow naturally as a vasodilator. Pineapple contributes its own phytochemical, bromelain, which scavenges the blood for impurities, toxins, and even dead or damaged blood cells. An added benefit of bromelain is its ability to dramatically improve the appearance of bruises by removing the dead and damaged blood cells beneath the surface of the skin that produce the appearance of a bruise.

Apple-Cucumber with Mint

Apples combine with cucumber and mint for a slightly sweet, mentholated infusion that helps to combat the chronic conditions that are commonly associated with men and women as they age.

Ingredients | Yields 1 liter

1 liter water
1 medium Fuji apple, peeled, cored, and sliced
3" piece cucumber, peeled and sliced
¼ cup mint leaves, chopped

1. Prepare a pitcher or water infuser product with 1 liter water.

2. Place the apple, cucumber, and mint inside the pitcher or water infuser's canister.

3. Allow mixture to steep in the refrigerator or a cool, dark place for 2–4 hours. For best flavor and health benefits, consume within 24–48 hours.

The Key Ingredients

Apples contribute vitamin C and its unique phytochemical, quercetin, to help strengthen the immune system and improve its ability to fight infection. Cucumber's potent phytochemicals, lignans, come to the rescue of the cells, helping to prevent and reverse free radical damage and maintain proper mental functions, such as memory, that can deteriorate with age. Finally, mint brings flavonoids that support antioxidant protection for cells of the brain, while providing the digestive system with calming anti-inflammatory agents that minimize digestive issues.

Sweet Cherry Green Tea with Ginger

The sweet and tart flavors of cherries get perfectly paired with the spiciness of ginger, combining to calm the traditionally tangy flavor of green tea, creating a delicious recipe that's sweet and subtly spicy.

Ingredients | Yields 1 liter
1 liter water
1 cup pitted cherries, chopped
1" piece ginger, peeled and sliced
2 organic green tea bags

1. Prepare a pitcher or water infuser product with 1 liter water.

2. Place the cherries, ginger, and tea bags inside the pitcher or water infuser's canister.

3. Allow mixture to steep in the refrigerator or a cool, dark place for 2–4 hours. For best flavor and health benefits, consume within 24–48 hours.

The Key Ingredients

As well as vitamin C, B vitamins, potassium, calcium, and magnesium, these ingredients provide antioxidants, anti-inflammatory agents, and phytochemicals to combat a variety of conditions—bacterial and viral infections, chronic respiratory conditions, and inflammatory digestive system conditions. Added to all that is the amino acid L-theanine, provided by green tea, which calms the brain while promoting proper communication between the nervous system and the brain and body.

Watermelon-Citrus Chamomile with Apple Cider Vinegar

Whether you sip this infusion morning, noon, or night, you can benefit from each of the ingredients in amazing ways that not only improve immunity and boost brain health, but also protect the cells and systems against harm and degradation.

Ingredients | Yields 1 liter
1 liter water
1 cup peeled and chopped watermelon
½ large lemon, peeled and sliced
2 chamomile tea bags
1 tablespoon organic, unfiltered, unpasteurized apple cider vinegar

1. Prepare a pitcher or water infuser product with 1 liter water.

2. Place the watermelon, lemon, tea bags, and vinegar inside the pitcher or water infuser's canister.

3. Allow mixture to steep in the refrigerator or a cool, dark place for 2–4 hours. For best flavor and health benefits, consume within 24–48 hours.

The Key Ingredients

Protein and amino acids present in the watermelon and tea promote protein synthesis, helping to support the maintenance of muscle mass and processing of minerals such as calcium that support bone density. The protective vitamin C from the lemon pairs with the enzymes of apple cider vinegar to boost the benefits to the immune system by protecting against infection and protecting the cells from oxidative stress and inflammation. Calming the brain and mind with the amino acid L-theanine, chamomile tea supports the brain's alpha activity, helping to reduce stress and restore peace.

Orange-Pomegranate

Tasting tangy and sweet, these fruits combine to provide support not only to the immune system but also to a system that struggles to maintain optimal levels of health as we age: the respiratory system.

Ingredients | Yields 1 liter

1 liter water
1 medium orange, peeled and sliced
½ cup pomegranate jewels, muddled

1. Prepare a pitcher or water infuser product with 1 liter water.

2. Place the orange and pomegranate inside the pitcher or water infuser's canister.

3. Allow mixture to steep in the refrigerator or a cool, dark place for 2–4 hours. For best flavor and health benefits, consume within 24–48 hours.

The Key Ingredients

The respiratory system's struggles with environmental and lifestyle-related toxic elements can increase over time, leading to chronic conditions that adversely affect the system's ability to fend off infection and function optimally. With both oranges' and pomegranates' provisions of vitamin C and powerful antioxidants, anti-inflammatory compounds, and natural analgesics, this recipe contributes nutrients that fight infections of bacterial and viral forms, prevent inflammatory responses, alleviate allergic reactions, and even minimize the pain most commonly associated with respiratory conditions.

Cherry-Pineapple-Blueberry

The sweetness of cherries, pineapple, and blueberries infuse every scrumptious sip of this recipe to maximize the flavor of your daily doses of water while providing the body and brain with protective vitamins, minerals, and antioxidants.

Ingredients | Yields 1 liter

1 liter water
½ cup pitted cherries, chopped
1 (½"-thick) slice of pineapple, peeled and chopped
¼ cup blueberries, lightly muddled

1. Prepare a pitcher or water infuser product with 1 liter water.

2. Place the cherries, pineapple, and blueberries inside the pitcher or water infuser's canister.

3. Allow mixture to steep in the refrigerator or a cool, dark place for 2–4 hours. For best flavor and health benefits, consume within 24–48 hours.

The Key Ingredients

Vitamins A, C, and E combine with calcium, potassium, magnesium, and silica to boost the antioxidant, anti-inflammatory, and antimicrobial benefits of each fruit in this recipe. These ingredients create a safeguard against cell degeneration and harmful oxidative stress that can wreak havoc on the body and mind. Preventing memory loss, possibly reducing the risk of Alzheimer's disease, and boosting brain functioning, this nutritious infused water recipe helps to maintain mental health for both men and women.

Spicy Cherry-Citrus

Thanks to the plentiful antioxidants provided by this recipe's ingredients, the entire body benefits from protection against the harmful oxidative stress and free radical damage that can wreak havoc on the cells, organs, and systems.

Ingredients | Yields 1 liter

1 liter water
½ medium jalapeño pepper, deseeded and sliced
½ cup pitted cherries, chopped
1 medium tangerine, peeled and sliced

1. Prepare a pitcher or water infuser product with 1 liter water.

2. Place the jalapeño, cherries, and tangerine inside the pitcher or water infuser's canister.

3. Allow mixture to steep in the refrigerator or a cool, dark place for 2–4 hours. For best flavor and health benefits, consume within 24–48 hours.

The Key Ingredients

Supporting the immune system with valuable doses of vitamin C, these ingredients also prevent the invasion of bacteria, viruses, and microbes that can degrade the functioning of the immune system or attack organs and systems. The respiratory system, cardiovascular system, muscular functioning, and bone density all benefit from the combination of vitamins, minerals, and antioxidants in this blend. Safeguarding the body from stress and degradation of all sorts while tasting great, this recipe makes for a spicy sweet treat.

Figs and Berries

The subtle sweetness of figs comes with a host of benefits from the potent provision of minerals including calcium and potassium. Helping to optimize the body's absorption of calcium and potassium, berries ensure that the body has these essential nutrients available to improve the health of bones and teeth.

Ingredients | Yields 1 liter
1 liter water
2 medium figs, peeled and sliced
¼ cup blackberries, lightly muddled
¼ cup raspberries, lightly muddled

1. Prepare a pitcher or water infuser product with 1 liter water.

2. Place the figs, blackberries, and raspberries inside the pitcher or water infuser's canister.

3. Allow mixture to steep in the refrigerator or a cool, dark place for 2–4 hours. For best flavor and health benefits, consume within 24–48 hours.

The Key Ingredients

Because osteoporosis and gingivitis are major health concerns for women as they age, this infused water recipe's nutrients specifically target these two health issues. With up to one-third of the daily recommended values of both calcium and potassium, the figs and berries in this blend combine to help women maintain optimal levels for bone density and oral health that can safeguard these areas of health throughout the years. These ingredients also provide antioxidants and anti-inflammatory compounds that help boost immunity, prevent infections of the respiratory system, reduce the incidence of chronic inflammatory conditions, and maintain mental health.

Acai-Orange with Mint

With cellular health being of the utmost importance in later years of life, it is essential for men and women to include nutrient-dense fruits in their daily diet. By consuming the nutrients infused into this delicious recipe, both men and women can help safeguard their health.

Ingredients | Yields 1 liter

1 liter water
½ cup acai berries, lightly muddled
1 medium orange, peeled and sliced
¼ cup mint leaves, chopped

1. Prepare a pitcher or water infuser product with 1 liter water.

2. Place the acai berries, orange, and mint inside the pitcher or water infuser's canister.

3. Allow mixture to steep in the refrigerator or a cool, dark place for 2–4 hours. For best flavor and health benefits, consume within 24–48 hours.

The Key Ingredients

With potent nutrition that acts to support brain function, nervous system health, and cardiovascular health, this recipe's fruits and mint help to keep the brain and body free of toxins and full of protective phytochemicals that act to protect cell health. Antioxidants, anti-inflammatory compounds, and essential vitamins and minerals such as B vitamins, vitamins A, C, and E, calcium, magnesium, and potassium make this recipe a delicious and nutritious way to combat illness, disease, and cellular degradation throughout life, regardless of age or gender.

Pomegranate-Pineapple Green Tea with Apple Cider Vinegar

Pomegranate jewels dazzle this recipe with their delightful shades of red and purple, contributing to this blend's nutrient-dense content that helps men and women achieve better cellular health.

Ingredients | Yields 1 liter

1 liter water
½ cup pomegranate jewels, muddled
1 (½"-thick) slice of pineapple, peeled and chopped
2 organic green tea bags
1 tablespoon organic, unfiltered, unpasteurized apple cider vinegar

1. Prepare a pitcher or water infuser product with 1 liter water.

2. Place the pomegranate, pineapple, tea bags, and vinegar inside the pitcher or water infuser's canister.

3. Allow mixture to steep in the refrigerator or a cool, dark place for 2–4 hours. For best flavor and health benefits, consume within 24–48 hours.

The Key Ingredients

Pomegranate and pineapple contribute anthocyanins, anthocyanadins, and bromelain for a detoxifying combination that keeps the blood free of toxins and cleansed of irregular, damaged, or dead blood cells. Green tea's natural provisions of catechins along with the naturally occurring enzymes of apple cider vinegar have several benefits: helping to prevent oxidative damage from free radicals, reducing inflammation caused by pro-inflammatory proteins, and boosting the pro-enzymatic contributions that support processes throughout the body (for example, in nutrient processing and production, and in nutrient storage, such as bones' maintenance of calcium stores).

Cranberry-Cantaloupe-Kiwi

Cranberries are a woman's best friend—they protect against the bad bacteria that can adhere to the urinary tract's walls and, if allowed to remain, can lead to the development of painful urinary tract infections that can spread to the kidneys.

Ingredients | Yields 1 liter

1 liter water
½ cup cranberries, crushed
½ cup peeled and chopped cantaloupe
1 medium kiwi, peeled and sliced

1. Prepare a pitcher or water infuser product with 1 liter water.

2. Place the cranberries, cantaloupe, and kiwi inside the pitcher or water infuser's canister.

3. Allow mixture to steep in the refrigerator or a cool, dark place for 2–4 hours. For best flavor and health benefits, consume within 24–48 hours.

The Key Ingredients

The cantaloupe contributes vitamin A, vitamin C, and magnesium, which can help to fight free radical damage to the cells throughout the body. Cantaloupes contribute massive benefits to the restoration and protection of eye health, such as in the condition of macular degeneration and the formation of cataracts. With its splendid dose of sweetness, the kiwifruit contributes cholesterol-regulating and respiratory-system-protecting antioxidants to help maintain a level of health that safeguards against the development of chronic conditions most commonly experienced as we age, regardless of gender.

Index